worth fighting for

Dana Vulin was born into a tight-knit family, with two older sisters and a twin brother. She and her family lived in the small community of Koolan Island off the coast of Western Australia during her early childhood, before relocating to Perth when Dana was six years old. On completing high school, Dana enrolled in a Bachelor of Communications at Edith Cowan University, where she graduated with majors in Advertising and Business Management.

DANA VULIN

worth fighting for

MICHAEL JOSEPH
an imprint of
PENGUIN BOOKS

MICHAEL JOSEPH

UK | USA | Canada | Ireland | Australia
India | New Zealand | South Africa | China

Penguin Books is part of the Penguin Random House group of companies
whose addresses can be found at global.penguinrandomhouse.com.

 Penguin
Random House
Australia

First published by Penguin Random House Australia Pty Ltd, 2017

10 9 8 7 6 5 4 3 2 1

Cover design by Alex Ross © Penguin Random House Australia Pty Ltd
Cover photograph by Julian Kingma
Picture section photograph (Dana Vulin and family outside court) © Theo Fakos / Newspix
Typeset in Sabon by Samantha Jayaweera, Penguin Random House Australia Pty Ltd,
and Midland Typesetters, Australia
Colour separation by Splitting Image Colour Studio, Clayton, Victoria
Printed and bound in Australia by Griffin Press, an accredited ISO AS/NZS 14001
Environmental Management Systems printer.

National Library of Australia
Cataloguing-in-Publication data:

Vulin, Dana, author.
Worth fighting for / Dana Vulin.
9780143797319 (paperback)

Vulin, Dana.
Victims of crimes – Rehabilitation – Biography.
Burns and scalds – Patients – Rehabilitation – Biography.
Stalking victims – Biography.
Survival.

penguin.com.au

CONTENTS

PROLOGUE

I was burnt because of my face. Because I was young and happy and full of life. A woman I didn't know grew jealous of me, then obsessed, then dangerous and, finally, murderous. Because I love life, another person decided that I didn't deserve to live.

But because I love life, I could not die.

I had so much to live for. To fight for.

I might never understand why it happened, or how another human being could do what was done to me. All I can tell you are the facts. That in the prime of my life I was engulfed by a living nightmare, one that took away my face, my body, my whole life. It took everything.

But I was born into a family and a world that taught me that love is stronger than hate, stronger than fear.

I was born into a family that taught me how to fight for the impossible. And so I did.

When the doctors told my family I would die, I lived. When they told me I would be lucky to survive, I thrived. When my body wanted to quit, when my heart stopped on the operating table, I would not let myself go. I would fight for my heartbeat, for my body, for my face, for everything the fire took away.

Because I knew my life was worth it. I knew it was worth fighting for.

chapter 1

PARADISE

You know how when you read a book about someone who's been through a huge struggle, or endured some unimaginable horror, they start out by talking about their life beforehand like they grew up in paradise? Well, there's no way around it. I grew up in paradise.

My dad, Don, who'd worked in mining ever since he'd arrived in Australia in the 1970s, got a job driving trucks on Koolan Island, a tiny iron ore–mining island off the coast of Western Australia. That was where we lived for the first part of my life: Mum, Dad, my two older sisters Svetlana and Suzie, and me and my twin brother Denis. When my mum, Vera, was due to give birth to Denis and me, she was transported to a hospital in Perth. Then we all got on a plane and flew 1900 kilometres, to live in this palm-tree paradise.

It was amazing, a tiny little town with beaches on all sides. We knew everyone on the island, but that wasn't hard – it was tiny. It is such a wonderful privilege to have had that childhood. Koolan Island was like its own little world, with palm trees and coconuts all around our house, and lizards and goannas escaping up the trunks when you went out into the backyard.

It was the best place you could imagine growing up in but, even back then, I wanted more out of life than that little slice of paradise could offer. There is only so much excitement you can find on an island. We had a VCR and I would watch the few tapes in our collection over and over. Some of them I never got sick of watching, like *The Little Mermaid*. I can still sing all the songs from it off by heart and it's one of my favourite movies, even today. Others, I got sick of. One time I won a VHS copy of *Back to the Future* and just watched it again and again, because there was nothing else to do. I trashed that tape; must have seen it a thousand times. I hate that movie so much these days – so sick of it – but I still love Disney.

There weren't many other kids to play with. My sisters were always just that little bit too old for me and would leave me out of their games. That would drive me crazy, so I would go and dob on them to Mum to get them into trouble.

'Just let her play with you!' Mum would scold them. So they'd be like, 'Sure.' And then a little later they'd call from Svet's room: 'Come and play with us, Dana!' I'd come running and they'd slam the door in my face, to teach me a lesson for being such a dobber. But then, of course, I had to dob on them for that. It was a vicious cycle.

Sometimes I would try teaming up with my twin brother, Denis, but that never worked out either. We would get in a fight and soon we'd start really smashing each other. My sisters would encourage it. They used to make us these little boxing rings and get us to basically face off against each other. But, out of me and my brother, I was always the tough one. I would fight to win. Later in life, our friends would joke that when we were in the womb our brains got switched, that I ended up with all the stereotypical male characteristics: a bit loud, a bit crude, extremely excitable.

When we were kids, he'd always end up losing our fights and then ganging up on me with my older sisters. It was never the twins against the older sisters; it was me against the world.

I had a lot of energy, even at that age – too much for our little island. I wanted to experience as much of life as I could, to see the world, talk to strangers, meet new people. I was always the centre of attention. My mum has a photo, taken when I was four years old, from this day we'd spent at the beach. Mum and Dad had been trying to nap in the sun and I'd been demanding they pay attention to me – with no luck. So, when she turned her back, I stole Mum's sunglasses from her purse and climbed up onto a plastic beach chair, put her giant eighties sunglasses on my face and posed like a classic Hollywood starlet: leaning back into the chair, legs crossed, fully working it for the camera.

'Mum! Look! Mum! Look at me!' Mum turned around and her eyes widened at the spectacle.

'Now take a photo!' I yelled.

She did, and I've still got that photo. I love it. I think it captures everything that was special about my family and the magical place I grew up in. What the photo doesn't show is that, seconds after Mum took it, while she was looking down and winding the film, I stripped off all my clothes and sat naked in the same pose.

'Mum! Take another photo!'

Like I said, I was always the centre of attention.

In 1992, we moved from the island back to Perth. There, I was reunited with Jackie, the daughter of a family friend who was born almost the same time as me, and who would become my best and oldest friend. We hit it off immediately, although we had our differences. She was still very much into younger girl stuff – toys, games, running around, wearing button-down shirts – while I'd started taking an interest in clothes and makeup. Jackie tells me that her first memory of us from primary school is me announcing I was going to give her a makeover and handing her a hair tie – before standing back and pulling out some tweezers and announcing that I was also going to have to do something about that monobrow.

I was always eager to be older than I was. Part of it was having two older sisters. Everyone naturally looks up to their older siblings, and I adored Svetlana and Suzie. I watched them grow up just a little bit ahead of me – start wearing makeup, get interested in fashion – and I wanted to be part of it all. After we returned to Perth, they took me under their wing a little more. And I stopped dobbing on them all the time – provided they shared their makeup and clothes with me.

Svetlana, especially, would help me out with outfits and advice. For a price. A couple of times she made me keep her room clean for two weeks to let me borrow a top from her. I always thought it was worth it, though. I didn't want to miss out on anything. For as long as I can remember, I've seen the world as mine for the taking, and I wasn't going to let a little hard work hold me back.

When I was ten, my parents split up. It wasn't one of those divorces where everyone is cool with it – it was a pretty unhappy time. But I was so lucky to have my brother and sisters, especially Svet, who was the sibling I lived with the most and who'd really been looking out for me since day one (when she wasn't trying to discipline me). Classic older sister. When my parents split, so did the family. Suzie went to live with my dad, Denis moved between both houses, and me and Svet went to live with Mum. It was sad, but it meant me and Svet grew closer than ever. In a lot of ways, she became something of a second mum. She was my sister, but also the person I could go to with any secret. She even stopped making me clean her room.

Because she was four years older than me, she went through all the important life stuff before I did, and so was be able to help me through it when I got there. Being the youngest meant that a lot of the battles had already been fought before my time. My folks started out strict but, by the time I came around, they'd chilled out. Suzie had taken most of the bullets: she got caught smoking, drinking, all that. Svet didn't; she didn't even get drunk for the first time until she was in her twenties. She was always the best behaved of us. So much so that my parents totally let their guard down and started to trust all their children much more. I got away with a lot more stuff than either of my sisters. As part of that, I was able to experience a lot of life, with Svet beside me every step of the way.

I got my period before all the other girls my age – when I was just eleven – and by the end of primary school I was taller than all the girls (and most of the boys) at my school. Maybe I should have been embarrassed, but Svet was like, 'Tall is good. Get even taller.' So I taught myself how to walk in heels. I was a natural – it was like I was always meant to wear them. Both Svet and Suzie helped me learn about fashion, but soon the student became the master. And helping me with fashion was only a tiny part of it. Svet did it all – uni, getting a job – before I did, and she was my guide to all those things when it was my turn.

When the time came to go to high school, I ended up in classes with one of my best friends, Stella. It was great. Jackie was enrolled somewhere else, which was sad, but I wasn't going to let that stop us from hanging out with her. One day, when Stella and I had the day off school and Jackie didn't, Jackie leant us a couple of her spare school-uniform shirts and we just went down to the other high school to chill out with her and her friends at lunchtime. We were hanging out, talking shit, making friends, and suddenly we got busted by one of the teachers. This teacher was furious and told us we were breaking the law and were in deep trouble, and started escorting us to the principal's office. Thinking quickly, I looked around me, and then made a decision.

'I'm gonna run,' I whispered to Stella.

'What?'

'Let's run. On my signal: one, two three.' And then we bolted – sprinting down the halls and out of the schoolyard while this poor teacher waddled after us, yelling. I was a bit worried some of the other kids would tell, but Jackie said later that there was no chance. Word had gone around the whole school and they all thought it was hilarious.

It wasn't that we were bad kids, we just weren't interested in wasting our time. Life is way too short to spend any of it in detention. We were young and we were going to make the most of that. It's a special time, when you are a young girl on the verge on womanhood, with your whole life ahead of you. I already knew I had a lot of life to live.

chapter 2

GROWING UP FAST

All through high school, I had lots of really close friends, but the trio of Stella, Jackie and me were super tight. We would hang out every chance we got, watch movies, go dancing, hit the shops. That's when I really started to pay attention to how I looked. I'd always loved clothes and makeup and all that came with it – when I was a little girl if my mum turned her back for a second I'd raid her makeup drawer. And then in primary school, when all the girls had the same schoolbag, I would customise mine and make it really punk and cool. Looking like everyone else was not for me. And as I was becoming a young woman, I took that to the extreme.

We started going out dancing when we were around fifteen or sixteen, and I would put together the most outrageous outfits. I couldn't stand the thought of looking the same as the woman next to me, so I mixed it up. One time we were going to a disco so I put on this matching blue suit, wore blue contacts, and set it all off by dyeing my hair bright red. I've always said I'm not interested in not standing out. My goal wasn't to look sexy – I wanted every outfit to have a talking point, something someone would want to ask me about.

I also had zero time for the idea of changing how I looked or how I acted because someone else didn't like it. I've never been the kind of person to judge someone I don't know. I don't really understand people who live their lives that way, or who go out of their way to hate on a stranger.

It's something I noticed when I was young. When our parents split up, there was a fair bit of gossip. Our community, Serbian and Macedonian people from the former Yugoslavia, was extremely tight-knit, but that meant that when bad news broke it could be a little bit intense with rumours and innuendo. Not long ago I'd been living on a tiny island, but sometimes Perth felt like a small island as well.

I got used to total strangers gossiping about me. I didn't let it bother me. If people want to judge me without getting to know me, that's hardly my problem. When I started going out to clubs, people would make assumptions about me from the second I walked in.

Years ago, I was hanging out in a club with Svetlana and we walked past these two women who looked me up and down. One of them said, just loud enough so that we could hear, 'Ugh, oh my god, check out this Barbie.'

Svetlana was pissed off too, but told me to leave it. I decided not to. I was going to have some fun. I went up to them, with my head tilted to the side, and started talking to them in the brightest, bubbliest, dumb-blondest voice I could muster.

'Hey, babes,' I burbled. 'How are youse?'

'Good.'

'Wow!' I kept shovelling the excited dumb blonde act onto them until they started playing nice. One of them told me she loved my earrings.

'Oh, thanks!' I giggled. 'They're Ver-sassy.'

'Um. It's actually pronounced Versace,' said one of the girls.

'No, it's definitely Ver-sassy.'

I insisted until they came around. They walked away and I like to think they went on pronouncing it wrong for the rest of their lives. Svetlana laughed for ages – but she got it. You can't hate on the haters, you just have to take the piss. I was walking in there knowing exactly who I was, with complete presence of mind. I'm no Barbie, even if I love my clothes. I didn't dress for attention from women or for men; I dressed for me. Some people just can't stand to see a woman comfortable in her own skin.

I've always taken people for who they are. I really believe that deep down people are trying their best, and if you give them a chance, they'll give you the best of themselves.

In 2003, I finished school with good grades, and then in 2005 I went to university to study communications, advertising and business management, and moved out of home for the first time. I rented a room in a share house with Danielle, a total stranger who came from a very different background to mine – her family was from England and she a little more quiet than me – but she would soon become one of my best friends. We were both busy with work and uni, and before long we would leave each other little presents and chocolates when we hadn't seen each other in a while. She was great cook and would spoil me with these awesome dinners. I tried to reciprocate, but, honestly, I've never been a great cook. The one time I tried to cook for her, she was sitting down all excited and I plonked down this hunk of meat that was burnt on the outside and frozen on the inside. Just totally inedible. And there's poor Danielle smiling and trying to force it down out of politeness. What a friend.

Later that year, me and some girlfriends went to see the Foo Fighters at Rock It festival, a big party in northern Perth that can get a bit loose. We were lining up for drinks and just in front of us there was this huge guy with tattoos, with all these drink tickets hanging out of his back pocket. Danielle tapped him on the shoulder and said, ever so sweet and polite, 'Excuse me, your tickets are hanging out of your pocket.'

This guy turned around and he just lost his mind. His face went blood-red and he started screaming, verbally attacking Danielle really outrageously, looming over her. Danielle shrank back, afraid he was going to punch her, and I jumped in between them and gave this guy a serve back.

'How dare you?' I demanded. 'What are you thinking? My friend here is just trying to help you not lose your drink tickets and you want to be rude to her, you arsehole? What's the matter with you?' I kept yelling at him while he seemed to visibly shrink. All the colour drained out of his face. Before long he apologised, and ended up giving Danielle all his drink tickets to say sorry. Back then I honestly believed nobody was really bad, not if you gave them a chance. I gave this guy a chance to not be a jerk and look what happened! Hostilities were ended and we got free drinks!

I wasn't a big drinker, though. I didn't really need alcohol; I just had unlimited energy. Lust for life. Every weekend me and my girlfriends would hit a circuit. We'd go to the Aberdeen, which is a bit of a cheesy club (and a Perth institution), then hit another club, and another, until we ended up at the Paramount, the last place open in town. My friends would be sitting on the floor, nodding off, and I'd still be up there chatting to people, ignoring any request to call it a night.

In those years at uni, I had the time of my life. Perth was in the middle of the mining boom and there was a bit of a Wild West vibe to the place. The mines flooded the whole city with cash and fascinating people from all over the world. All of whom had an interesting story to tell, something to share or teach you. Through those years, I kept my open-mindedness and made friends from all over the globe, from all walks of life. By the time I finished uni, I was close with classmates, people I'd met at clubs, even my university professors. Some of them were quite conservative, naturally – but I also had a lot of time for people from more alternative backgrounds.

One really good friend of mine, Milesy, this magnificent sweetheart, just the most amazing person, was also kind of intimidating-looking. Huge, muscles, tattooed – he used to like to party, rolled with a few bikies. When I introduced him to my girlfriends, they were like, 'Are you kidding?' But I scolded them for judging him based on who he hung around with and how he looked. We ended up all partying together, making some really precious memories, and he always had our backs. Sadly, he's since passed away, but the girls are grateful that I convinced them to keep an open mind. I just loved meeting people. Of course, being so open-minded didn't always work out. There were times I was maybe a little more open-minded than I should have been.

By 2011, I'd finished uni with a double degree and picked up awards for excellence in marketing and strategic design. I got a great job in the field and, for the first time in my life, I had a grown-up income. With the money that brought in I could afford a place all of my own, so

I stopped share-housing and moved into a little apartment in a swish new complex, not far from the casino. Ever since I was a little girl, I'd felt like the world was my oyster, and now, after a years of hard work, it was.

I loved that flat and kitted it out in full Dana style. As much as I'd loved living with my girlfriends, there really was nothing like having my own place to go back to and chill, or to have people over.

Occasionally, I'd hang out with people who maybe partied a little too hard, who dabbled in recreational substances. I was young, I was having fun – and I made mistakes, some bad decisions.

One time I was partying when the police turned up at my apartment. That was the end of that party. Like a lot of young people, I used drugs a couple of times, but never thought I'd be in trouble with the police. It was mortifying – and a real wake-up call.

I spoke to a lawyer about what to do. They told me not to worry, that it was a simple matter of turning up to court, explaining what had happened, and it would all be sorted. I agreed, as the last thing I wanted was for this thing to get out of hand. I promptly ditched the dudes who'd led me down that path. I knew I had to put it behind me, change my ways; there was no time in my life for that nonsense.

Besides, I had recently found the love of my life. His name was Killer.

When I met him he was still a puppy, a tiny little golden purebred longhaired chihuahua. I'd decided I wanted a pet and at first I was on the lookout for a kitten. Playful, cute, but independent; I liked their style.

But when I saw Killer, it was all over.

He was from a litter of five, but the only one with hazel eyes. I saw those eyes and I was a goner. Bright peepers sticking out of this tiny little ball of white fur. I paid the breeder and drove home with Killer. It was three hours back to Perth and by the time I got home, that was it. I had fallen in love. I was already a stage-5 clinger, total desperado.

From that minute, we went everywhere together. I would take him with me to the shops, to cafes, to parties, everywhere I went. It got to the point where if I went somewhere without him, people would be disappointed. I'd turn up to dinner to meet Danielle, and the first thing she'd say would be, 'Where's Killer? Is he okay?'

'He's fine,' I'd say. 'And I'm good too, thanks for asking.'

Before long I was referring to him as my son, and he kind of was – just cruising around under my arm, 24/7. As he got bigger my arm started to get tired, so I went to a store to check out baby carriers. I was trying one on when this woman started chatting to me about her baby.

'They are so wonderful at this age, aren't they?' she cooed.

'Yep, totally.'

'Mine's only four months. How old is yours?'

'He's . . . still little.'

He was little, but he had attitude. He wasn't naughty, not exactly, but if I came home at night and went to sleep without playing with him, I'd wake up and my best shoes would be chewed up. He'd be sitting there, all calm, looking me right in the eye like, 'Take that!' I don't know how he always knew which pair of shoes was the most expensive in my wardrobe. I guess he just had good taste, like his mum. Every time he'd wreck a pair of shoes, I'd laugh it off. 'It's good that he's got a vicious side,' I would joke. 'He's my little attack dog, my security system.'

Looking back now, that joke maybe isn't as funny as I thought it was. But then, who could have known what was about to happen? Who in their wildest nightmares could have anticipated what came next?

chapter 3

THE STALKER

It was New Year's Eve, 2011, and I was out with my girl-friends at Crown Casino in Perth. We'd celebrated the new year with champagne and fireworks, and then hit the casino, one of the few venues open late at night. At this point I was just twenty-five, in the prime of my life, young, independent, professional, with a loving family. I had it all. Looking back, there was nothing out of the ordinary, no hint that everything was about to change.

We'd had a few drinks, won a few times at the black-jack tables, and I was lining up to cash my chips when the guy behind me struck up a conversation.

'Do I know you from somewhere?' he asked.

As far as pick-up lines go it wasn't terribly original, but it wasn't the worst I'd heard. In those days, I got a lot of attention from men. It was no big deal. I was happy to chat, always happy to meet new people, even if I wasn't looking for romance. And that night, I definitely wasn't. I'd been seeing this guy Paul – nothing serious, but we were hanging out and having fun. Besides, this guy talking to me in the casino was not my type at all.

'I'm sure I know you from somewhere,' he repeated. 'How do I know you?'

'I don't know. What's your name?'

'Edin. Edin Handanovic.'

He seemed nice enough, and he did look a little familiar, so we started chatting. His name sounded Yugoslav and, as my heritage is half Macedonian, half Serbian, I'd grown up in the community. I thought maybe he recognised me as a friend of a friend of a friend. Maybe he'd seen me across the room at a party or something.

'That must be it. I must have seen you around,' he decided. We chatted for about half an hour, if that: 'Happy New Year' and 'how's so-and-so', that kind of thing. The conversation was totally innocent. He seemed like the least sleazy guy you might meet at the casino in the middle of the night. He mentioned he'd recently separated from his wife and I gave him my sympathies. At the time, it was a totally unremarkable conversation – but it turned out to be one that would ruin my life. One of those random, seemingly tiny events that changes everything.

The first phone call was less than a month later. It was Australia Day 2012 and I was at a barbecue with friends when my mobile rang.

'Dana?' A woman's voice, one I'd never heard before.

'Hi, yes. Who's this?'

'This is Natalie.'

'Who?'

'Edin's wife.'

It took me a minute to figure out who she meant, then I remembered meeting Edin, the guy at the casino on New Year's Eve. 'Oh, right. Okay. How's it going?'

'I'm calling to let you know me and Edin are back together.'

'Okay, great. I'm happy for you.' At this point, I was a little baffled as to why she was calling, and I wanted to get back to the party. 'Is there something I can help you with?'

That's when her tone changed.

'You'd better be scared, bitch.'

'. . . what?'

'I know all about you. I know what you've done. I know you're fucking my husband.'

I was startled, obviously, but that was just the start. She proceeded to abuse me as I listened, shocked, and her voice got louder and angrier until she was screeching and I could barely understand her. Natalie called me a slut, a bitch, a fucking cunt. She said I had better be scared because she was going to smash my fucking head in and kill me. Then she hung up.

I was stunned. I'd never met the woman, as far as I could remember, and I'd never so much as kissed her husband on the cheek. After thinking about it for a while I decided to call her back. I thought that if I could explain that clearly she'd misunderstood the situation, whatever idea she'd got into her head would be gone and she would feel better. She didn't pick up, so I wrote a text to the number in my phone's call history, wishing her and Edin a long and happy life. I asked her to please not call me again because I wanted nothing to do with her, and nothing to do with Edin. The message sent, and I went back to enjoying the barbecue.

The next call was just over a week later, 3 February, this time from a private number.

'Hello?'

'Dana? It's Natalie.'

'Who?'

'Natalie.'

'Ugh.' Not this again. I hung up. I had no interest in being abused by this woman. I felt sorry that she was having whatever these problems were, but it was none of my business. She immediately rang back, but I let it go to voicemail. Over the next two weeks she called me a dozen times, always from private or random numbers. Whenever I picked up she would be in the middle of a screaming fit, in the vilest rage you could imagine, and it was always some iteration of the same conversation.

'Hello, this is Dana.'

'Where is he, you fucking slut? You're fucking dead, cunt, you hear me, you're fucking dead!'

Click. I hung up each time, baffled by this surreal and slightly unnerving development in my life.

It was clear that this woman was delusional and probably mentally unwell. I tried to figure out what had happened. Someone must have told her that I'd been talking to her husband at the casino, and she'd assumed there was something more to that innocent conversation. To this day, I have no idea why she fixated on me.

I hoped she would figure out the truth, or get bored and leave me alone, but no luck. The calls just kept coming. In the end, I decided to try and reason with her. One day, taking a big breath, I picked up one of her calls and answered in my calmest voice.

'Where is he?' she demanded. 'Put him on.'

'What are you talking about?

'Edin. I know he's staying with you so just put him on.'

It was time to sort out this craziness, and I spoke to her calmly, like I would a child throwing a tantrum. 'Natalie, I don't know where he is. I haven't seen him for weeks.'

'You're lying. I know he's there with you.'

'Look, Natalie, he's not. It would be easier for me to just tell you he's here since, whatever I say, you don't believe me anyway. I'm sorry, but the truth is, I haven't seen him.'

She thought this over for a second, and shot back with, 'So if you haven't seen him, prove it by meeting up with me.'

'What?'

'Meet up with me now. I'll meet you at the casino.'

'I'm not meeting up with you.'

She seemed to take this as proof of my wrongdoing. 'I knew it! Why not? What are you hiding?'

'It's the weekend, I have plans. Why would I cancel them to meet up with someone who's threatening my life? Someone who, frankly, is acting quite crazy?' At this point, she lost it entirely and started to scream in a completely unhinged way.

'Do you know who I am? Do you know what I've done? What I can do to you? Who you've made enemies with? Don't go anywhere or do anything, because I will find you and kill you. You've made yourself the worst enemy you could. You hear me? I'm going to ruin your pretty little face!' Her voice was still going, mid-rant, when I hung up.

It's hard to articulate what I was feeling at that point. I was completely unnerved. You can't listen to someone threaten your life without having your heart try to leap out of your chest. And it wasn't what she said – although the content was horrific – but the *way* she said it that really spooked me. It was at once crazy and calm, completely unhinged but determined. The tone she used was something far beyond anger. It was chilling.

On one occasion, I received ten phone calls from Natalie in the same day. I ignored the ones I knew were from her, but when a strange number came up, I took it.

'Hello, is this Dana Vulin?' It was a strange voice, a man's.

'Yeah. Who's this?'

'Do you like cock, you little slut?'

'What?'

'I bet you do. You're going to get raped and you're going to love it. And then we're going to ruin your pretty little face.'

I was shocked and scared. And angry. 'Who is this? What do you want?'

'We're watching you. We can see you right now'

I looked around my apartment, unsettled. 'Who's we?' I demanded. On the other end of the line, I heard the phone being passed to another person, and then Natalie's now familiar voice.

'You hear him, bitch? We're coming for you.' She hung up.

I was now starting to feel really uneasy. Apart from everything that was happening with the phone calls, I was getting other warning signs from different corners of my life. Two girlfriends had called, warning me that someone called Natalie was on the warpath, that she had been to their houses and pretty much kicked their doors down looking for me. Another heard rumours that Natalie was a tweaker, an ice addict, and that she was hanging around my neighbourhood offering an ounce of crystal meth for my address. That was a very disturbing thing to hear.

After this latest phone call, I sat for a moment staring at my phone, wondering what to do?

'*Call the police*,' said a voice somewhere in the back of my mind.

'*And tell them what?*' came the reply. What *would* I tell them? That I was getting horrible phone calls from someone I'd never even laid eyes on? For no reason? What could they even do about that?

'*Call Svet*,' the voice said next. Through my whole life, she'd been the one I turned to whenever I had a problem. From school, to boys, to work, she had a way of giving really solid advice that let me figure out the way forward. If anyone would know what to do in this crazy situation, it would be her.

But how could I describe this bizarre problem to her? What use is good advice in the face of double-barrelled insanity? And I really didn't want to worry her. She'd just had a baby a couple of weeks ago, and she had bigger things to deal with than this. I'd faced belligerent crazies before and I'd always managed to talk them down. I thought about the giant, red-faced dude from Rock It festival all those years ago, and thought that this woman couldn't possibly be worse news than him.

Honestly, I was more than just a little scared. But I was a confident woman and I thought I could handle it. I was fit, and if I ever found myself in danger, I was sure I could escape. When I went out at night I carried something to protect myself. I had a can of pepper spray that I kept zipped up in a side pocket of my bag, where I could easily reach it if anything went down.

The evening of 10 February, I was hanging with a friend of mine called Luke Richardson, who worked as a fly-in-fly-out worker in the mines. He was due to fly back out soon, so we were catching up as much as we could. I'd confided to him about the phone calls, as he'd been with me when one happened, and he did his best to reassure me there was nothing to worry about.

'Don't stress,' he told me. 'Nothing is going to happen. They're just crazy and trying to make you paranoid.'

When Natalie rang that night, he took the phone and firmly and calmly told her that nothing was going to happen to me, not on his watch. I could hear Natalie starting to scream at him through the phone, so he yelled as loud as he could into the microphone: 'Bring it on then! I'm not scared of you! I don't care if you're watching!'

He started stomping around the apartment pretending to check in the cupboards and behind doors, like a dad pretending to look for the boogieman to reassure a child. He finished up by walking out onto the balcony and screaming out into the night, at the top of his lungs, 'Come on, then!' I laughed, and Natalie's behaviour seemed less threatening and more ridiculous, so I thanked him and then let him go home without a second thought.

I had an appointment early the next day at the magistrate's court, to sort out the consequences of the police finding the drugs in my house. I wanted to put everything right as quickly as possible. The lawyer I spoke to assured me that it was nothing serious, I just needed to turn up, show my face in court, and everything would be settled. But it did mean I had to be up at the crack of dawn.

I felt safe being alone in my apartment, despite all of Natalie's threats, because it boasted all sorts of fancy security measures. That was part of the reason I'd chosen the place – and was paying top dollar for it. My mum, who is a very emotional person, was a little bit heartbroken when I announced I was moving out on my own. She worried about my safety, and so it gave her peace of mind for me to be able to demonstrate the safety features.

'Look at this place!' I'd reassured her. 'You'd need a tank to get in here.'

To get into my building, you needed to get past a security door with an electronic lock wired to a video intercom. The only other access to the building was through an underground car park, which had a separate security system. Basically, there was no way in or out of the building unless you had a key card or were with one of the tenants. I'd never felt in danger there.

So when I heard a knock at the door, not long after Luke had left, I opened it without hesitating. I assumed it was either a neighbour or the apartment manager. They were the only ones who could get in without a key card. But it wasn't.

The door flung open and I jumped back as a strange woman pushed her way past me into the apartment. She was dressed in black, with olive skin and long blonde hair. She was about my height and moved with a kind of restless, intense energy.

She ran straight past me, forcing herself further into my apartment and towards my bedroom, yelling, 'I know you're in here!'

I immediately recognised the voice as the one that had been screaming abuse at me down a phone line for the past two weeks. 'Natalie? Are you Natalie?'

She ignored me and continued checking through my house – every room, in the shower, behind doors, just like Luke had done before as a joke. I wasn't laughing now, though. It was clear she was looking for her husband. 'Natalie! He's not in here, get out!'

Until she'd thoroughly checked the whole apartment, she ignored me, like I wasn't standing right next to her. It was completely surreal. I was astonished by the intrusion, but probably not as scared as I should have been. If anything, I was annoyed. Who did this woman think she was, forcing her way into my home? I kept my cool and tried to think of the best way to resolve and defuse what was happening.

I had nothing to hide, and at that stage I figured that if she needed a confrontation, I would give her one. Maybe this would finally sort out all this craziness. If she could see for herself that I had no idea where her husband was then surely she would listen to reason. I waited until she stopped, and she sat down on my couch and lit a cigarette.

'You can't smoke in here,' I told her. 'Take it outside.' She nodded, and together we went to stand on the balcony. Natalie seemed a little calmer, and so I said to her, 'You see? He's not here.'

'Do you know where he is?'

'No.'

'He's been hiding from me,' Natalie said, and while part of me was thinking, '*I don't blame him*,' I did feel kind of sorry for her. She clearly wasn't very well, emotionally. It seemed like she'd truly believed she would find Edin hiding in my wardrobe, like in some kind of soap opera.

She told me that if I wanted her to believe I wasn't seeing her husband behind her back, I should give her my phone so she could call his number. If his number wasn't in my phone, that was evidence in my favour. I didn't see the harm, so I handed over my phone and she dialled his home number and put it on loudspeaker. Edin's father answered, saying he hadn't seen his son, didn't know where he was, and that he wouldn't be home for a while.

After that, Natalie seemed to calm down. She seemed to believe that I hadn't seen or heard from Edin since our chance meeting on New Year's Eve. She told me he was mixed up in some bad stuff and that some guy called Peppy was looking to bash him, so maybe that's why he was in hiding. I did what I could to be sympathetic, but I was very tired of Natalie and her delusions, so I tried to hustle her out the door.

'You really need to go, Natalie.'

'But what if Peppy finds Edin?'

I tried to reassure her. 'I'm sure it's fine. I'm sure Edin can look after himself. This Peppy guy can't be so tough.'

She froze and stopped halfway to the door. 'What do you know about Peppy?'

'You just told me about him.'

'Did Edin talk to you about Peppy? And the bashing? When you met on New Year?'

I shrugged. 'Maybe, I don't know.'

'Nah, no way.' She flipped, 180 degrees, from calm to screaming right in my face at the top of her lungs. 'He bashed Peppy after that, and you told me you hadn't seen him since long before that.'

'I haven't!'

'Liar!' She repeated the world, screaming it like some kind of demented prayer. 'Liar, liar!'

'I'm not lying. We've had, like, one conversation.'

It went on like this for a while, back and forth. Her screaming 'liar!' in my face while I told her to get out. I managed to get us both downstairs into the underground car park. Much to my surprise, I saw that her car was parked directly opposite mine. This meant that she knew not only my address but that she knew how to get past the security in the car park. It also explained how she managed to get all the way to my front door without any trouble. She couldn't have done any of that unless she had the help of someone who knew me, which was a disturbing thought. I didn't have time to ask her, though, because she was already climbing into her car and driving off, still furious.

The whole incident was nasty. As much as I hoped it would calm things down, they were left quite unsettled. Natalie was angrier than ever and, as it turned out, she'd made me late for my court appointment. When I turned up, the magistrate had already called my case. I was in trouble for being a no-show. After a great deal of nego-tiation, I managed to get an opportunity to have another hearing, but I was warned that if I missed this one, a warrant would be put out for my arrest.

I left the courtroom fuming about Natalie. She'd ruined my chance to do the right by thing by the courts, so when she called later that day I picked up immediately.

'How do you know where I live, Natalie?' I demanded.

'Why would I tell that to a liar?' She was still hostile, but in a different way now, almost playful.

'I've told you, I'm not a liar, and I haven't seen your ex-husband. You're delusional and you need help. Now tell me where you got my address.'

'One of your friends told me.'

'Who?'

'Nah . . . only jokes.' She laughed. This really weird, high-pitched giggle. 'I knew you lived near the casino, so I just drove around the neighbourhood and asked if they knew where the blonde lived. These guys in your building let me in and I shouted them ice-pipes and they told me everything.'

I suspected this was untrue. I didn't live in a building full of drug users, and besides, she'd known every detail of the car park. So I called her a liar, which only set her off again. She accused me again of lying about Edin and called me a slut, to which I responded calmly and coolly.

'Natalie, Edin's not my type. He's way shorter than me for starters, and also, I think he's ugly.'

I probably shouldn't have said that, because it made her really angry.

'You're fucking dead, bitch. I'm going to kill you. But first I'm gonna ruin your pretty little face.' Then she hung up.

I hoped that was the last I would hear from her, and the phone calls did stop. After a while, I pushed Natalie and all her delusional, crazy behaviour to the back of my mind. I had a life to lead, and I wasn't the kind of woman who let bullies bring down my mood.

At the time Paul, the guy I was seeing, would often hang around the apartment with me – so if she came to my home again, chances were he'd be there. And besides, I was young and fit, so if she became physically violent, I was sure I'd be able to handle her. The second she raised a finger to me, I would have called the cops and that would be that.

If I'd known what was coming I would have been so much more scared. I would have run a million miles.

chapter 4

THE ATTACK

In the early hours of 16 February, I woke up to the sound of Natalie in my house.

I'd fallen asleep on the couch. It was a hot night and I'd drifted off without a top on – wearing only loose army pants that came halfway down my calves. Across from me stood Natalie, with her arms crossed, wearing black pants, a black singlet and a black hat.

'Hello, Dana,' she said as I opened my eyes.

She'd watched the place until Paul left, sitting in her car for hours upon hours, smoking drugs, waiting for the chance to make her move. I would find all that out, but only much later, when it was far too late.

She'd forced her way in through the sliding doors from the private balcony at the back of my unit. The lock on the door had been broken for a couple of weeks.

I'd locked myself out of the apartment and had only been able to get back in by climbing onto my balcony from the side of the building. I would later learn that was how Natalie got in as well. I'd been keeping the sliding door sealed by jamming a piece of wood into the track that it opened along, but it was still possible to open it about 30 centimetres or so, enough for Natalie, skinny as she was, to squeeze through.

I got up, shocked, and covered my boobs with my arms. 'Natalie!' I yelled, 'what the fuck are you doing? Get out of my house!' She just stood grinning at me, eyes wide and glassy. She was high.

'Where is he?' Natalie asked.

I was still groggy. 'What do you mean?'

'My husband,' she demanded. 'I know he's here.'

I had no idea what she was talking about. Still half-asleep, I got to my feet and stumbled about, looking for something to put on, and finally found a top on my bed. As I was struggling into it I heard the wood keeping the balcony door closed being removed and the sliding door being pulled all the way open. I walked back into the living area and found Natalie had let someone else into the apartment, a tall, heavily built guy.

The man stooped down and was playing with my dog, Killer. I had no idea who this guy was at the time, but later I'd find out his name was Daniel Stone. He was not a friendly looking person in the slightest. His eyes, like Natalie's, were widened by drugs, and cold. He was grinning, but his smile was awful – cruel like his eyes, and smug in a really chilling way. He knelt down to keep playing with Killer. I didn't like that, because my little dog was everything to me. As if sensing my discomfort, the man looked up at me and winked.

'Just tell me where my husband is,' Natalie screamed, and I realised that she thought I was hiding Edin somewhere. I tried to reason with her. At this point I still thought that if I could just calmly explain to Natalie that I wasn't having an affair with her husband then the misunderstanding would clear itself up and she would leave. The whole thing was so ridiculous to me. I had no interest in the man whatsoever, I had barely even met him, but I could not make Natalie understand that. She was ranting, demanding I produce her husband out of thin air.

I moved across the room to give myself space, putting the bench that divided the kitchen area from the lounge room between us, because she wasn't calming down. She ranted and raved at me while, in the background, Daniel Stone calmly took a phone call. He looked almost bored.

At that point, Natalie noticed the glass candle on my dining room table. She snatched it up. It was a methylated-spirits burner, a kind of candle made of clear glass where the wick draws fuel from the chamber within. I'd bought the candle for a bit of mood lighting in my apartment, but Natalie had other ideas. She held it tight, lit it, and then whipped out a glass crack pipe and used the candle to start heating up a rock of crystal meth. I couldn't believe it.

As the sharp, chemical smell filled up my apartment, it occurred to me that this was the behaviour of a proper ice addict.

She'd probably been high every time she'd called me. It would explain her irrational behaviour, her paranoia, her threats. Ice addicts live in an entirely different world, one with different rules. Ice lets users stay awake for days and days upon end. While the body doesn't get tired, the mind slowly starts to unravel, and people can become aggressive, irrational, and violent. After days without sleep a person can enter a state of psychosis. That's when the really terrifying potential of the drug is unlocked: a user can enter a state of total delusion, fixating on fantasies, carrying out the most frightening actions, all without stopping to think about what they are doing. Much later, in court, it would be revealed that Natalie and Stone had been watching my house all night, smoking crack pipe after crack pipe, waiting to catch me alone. When Paul had left that night, they'd seen their chance.

In that moment, though, I'd had more than enough. I moved across the room to snatch the burner off her. The naked flame flickered between us as I demanded she get out of my house. 'He's not here, Natalie!' I was yelling in frustration now. 'Take a look around. He's not here! I don't even know him!'

Stone finished his phone call and moved to stand behind Natalie. She looked over her shoulder to talk to him.

'What do you think, Stoney?'

'You know what I think,' he said. 'I think the bitch is full of shit.'

It was only then that I realised how much danger I was in. I remembered all the threatening calls from Natalie and the strange man. I recognised the voice – it was this man. The one who'd said, 'I'm going to rape you. I'm going to mess up your pretty face. *I'm going to kill you.*'

I was terrified now. Taking the burner, I retreated back behind the kitchen bench, close to the front door, putting some distance between us in case Stone made a move towards me. But it was Natalie who moved forward. She was less than a metre away, and getting frantic.

'Just tell me where he is,' she threatened, 'or I'm going to burn you!'

This seemed so ridiculous I almost laughed, but instead I just cried, 'What for, Natalie? What did I ever do to you?'

A second later my life as I knew it was over.

Natalie grabbed a bottle of methylated spirits from the cleaning products on my kitchen bench, removed the cap and threw the liquid all over me. Waving her hand in a zig-zagging motion, she doused me with the chemical, hitting my face, arms, chest, everything from the waist up. The methylated spirits caught the naked flame in my hand and suddenly the whole world was on fire.

The flames were everywhere: my shoulders, my naked stomach – only my boobs were protected by my tiny boob tube. The flames spread to my head, my hair went up in seconds, and when I reached up to wipe the burning chemicals off my face, my hands were already on fire. Panic took hold of me and I dropped to the floor to try to smother the flames.

My mind went back to a classroom years and years ago, when Constable Care, a cartoonish puppet who taught kids basic safety principles, visited our school. It's something that every Perth schoolchild remembers: this big friendly puppet telling you to look both ways before you cross the street, to be wary of stranger danger, and, if you find yourself on fire, to stop, drop and roll.

So, in the moment, that's what I did.

This turned out to be the worst possible thing I could have done – a big no-no for chemical burns. When I hit the floor and rolled around, all I managed to do was spread the burning chemicals onto my back, so now I was engulfed by flames. The pain was excruciating, but through my screaming I could hear Natalie and Daniel making their escape through the sliding door.

They were laughing at me while I burnt alive.

When I stood up the flames were getting worse, and I could barely think through the pain. Panicked, I turned to the sink, trying to put the flames out by pouring a bucket of water over myself. I kept screaming for help, for anybody who could hear. Across the room, poor little Killer was whining in terror.

I knew that I needed to get help. I was as good as dead without it. As I fumbled with the front door I could feel the skin falling from my fingers. I managed to get the door open and crossed the hallway to the unit next to mine, kicking at the door while yelling for help. Long moments passed. There was no answer.

Even after the fire was finally extinguished the chemicals continued burning me and it was so intense. I screamed so loud and for so long that when someone finally came, he wasn't even my neighbour. The guy who turned up was working out in the gym of an apartment building next to mine, and he'd heard my screams and come running. By the time he got to me the flames had gone out. There was little left for them to burn. I lay dying on the floor. I opened my eyes to find a man in gym gear squatting next to me.

'I'm Denis,' he said, in a voice so calm it immediately brought me out of my state of shock a little bit. 'I'm here to help.'

I'll say this about Denis Ericson: the man is a hero. He lives in another building and he's the one who saved me. Think about it: from inside the gym of another building he hears a woman in distress and comes running, takes charge, saves her life. There's nothing about that day I'd wish on anyone, but it makes me feel so happy for humanity that there are people like Denis around – calm, kind, and heroic.

'What happened?' he asked.

'I've been set on fire,' I choked out.

He took charge immediately. 'We need to get you in the shower,' he said, helping me up, but I tried to argue.

'Please, no,' I begged. I was in shock, and I believed that running a burn under water is what made it blister. I fought with Denis as he kept convincing me to walk to the shower; I was terrified that if he put me under the water it would disfigure me completely.

I could see it in my mind so clearly, the damage the shower would inflict on me. Looking back with what I know now, it's just about the dumbest thing I could have thought. Denis was great, so calm, and spoke to me really nicely to get me into the shower. Asking me my name, telling me everything would be okay, that help was on the way, to just hang in there and that everything would be alright.

Inside my ensuite, Denis turned on the cold-water tap and helped me crouch down under the stream. Even though the water was only on a gentle trickle, every drop felt like a tiny knife straight onto the exposed nerve endings where my skin had been burnt away.

I could see the entire upper half of my body was ruined. My hands were the worst – I remember looking at them as they curled into useless little fists before my eyes. I wept.

The pain was unbearable. Denis stood beside me in the shower trying to comfort me. 'Everything is going to be okay. Help is in on the way. Just hang in there, it won't be long and we'll have help here. You're going to be alright.'

I stayed conscious, in agony, until the ambulance got there and the emergency workers came into the room, my tiny ensuite full of police, firemen and paramedics, who put me onto a stretcher and into an ambulance. 'Knock me out,' I remember yelling to the paramedics. 'Please, the pain – please, just knock me out.'

Weeks later, when it became clear I would never be able to live in my apartment again, my family came by to pack up my home. Svet organised for everything to be put in storage – my bed, my clothes, all that I owned. Then she cleaned the place for the next tenant, repairing the damage from the fire. Years later she told me the hardest part was while she was cleaning those tiles from my bathroom, weeping as she scraped the dead skin off the floor of the shower.

The pain before I finally passed out in the ambulance was worse than anything I could ever have imagined – but that would turn out to be a tickle compared to what lay ahead of me.

chapter 5

HOSPITAL

When you've been burnt alive, a lot of things change, physically and emotionally. But some things don't. I've always tried to look on the bright side – I believe that there's always a silver lining if you look hard enough. In this case, it's that I happened to live just down the road from one of the best hospitals on the planet for burns treatment. Two minutes after Denis called the ambulance they were at my house, and four minutes after that I was in the Royal Perth Hospital, which is home to Australia's best burns unit.

Professor Fiona Wood, who is a legend in the field of burns treatment, is based there. She developed spray-on skin technology and was named Australian of the Year in 2005. The team she's built is made up of far and away the best medical professionals someone who's been badly burnt could hope to have. Whenever someone in Western Australia needs specialist burns treatment, they are flown to Fiona and her team.

The ambulance carried me into the emergency department and immediately the whole hospital scrambled to save my life. The doctors had never seen someone with their body burnt so badly. The prognosis wasn't good. Even for these brilliant surgeons, the best in the world, my wounds were horrifying.

They saw that my burns were not only extensive but terribly deep – parts of my skin were destroyed all the way down to the muscle beneath. Everyone was mobilised: the emergency department, the anaesthetic staff, the intensive-care staff and the team of burns specialists. In all, twenty people rapidly assembled to try to keep me alive long enough to stabilise me. Every single one of them was the best in the world, and in my eyes, a hero, but leading them was Professor Suzanne Rea, a legend in her field and one of the world's most visionary burns surgeons. She was in the middle of another operation but was called out to help me. In time she would become a friend, a mentor and an inspiration – a truly kind and caring guide on my journey back from hell. But that day she was just a professional on top of her game, with a massive medical emergency to deal with.

'Your burns were some of the worst I'd ever seen,' she told me later. 'To treat an injury of that size requires a very invasive operation straight away, but we had to make sure you were well enough to undergo it.'

I was put into an induced coma and covered from head to toe in protective gel and bandages. At that point, now that I was no longer actually on fire and the doctors had removed my burnt skin tissue, the most imminent danger was infection. One of the major functions of your skin is to protect you from foreign objects, including viruses and other pathogens. There are billions and billions of bacteria crawling across your body all the time and it's the skin that keeps them out. I'd just lost more than half of mine. Without that natural defence, the bugs could have a field day. In cases as severe as mine, the bacteria can get through the burnt skin within two hours. Within four, it can become a major problem, and for me, it did.

'You got very sick,' is how Suzanne Rea puts it, bluntly. 'Very septic – the amount of damaged tissue and the infection associated with that was profound and life threatening.'

My burns were just too extensive, providing too large an area for germs to infiltrate. Soon, on top of everything else, I had a spiking infection that was threatening to kill me, and it was touch and go from minute to minute whether or not my body would give up the fight. The technical term was septic shock, a serious medical condition that happens when physical damage leads to infected blood, dangerously low blood pressure and crazy changes to metabolism as the immune system overloads. It was always going to be a major risk with the sheer amount of damaged tissue and the potential for infection that comes with that sort of an insult to the system. That's what doctors call it, an insult, and let me tell you: that's a serious understatement. It hurts like hell.

I would have certainly died if it weren't for Denis and for the ambulance workers who rushed to my aid. I was so very lucky that they responded to my attack with lightning speed.

Unfortunately, so did the media. As the world's finest burns doctors struggled to stabilise me, the story was already breaking in newsrooms across the city. Radio stations in Perth ran the news in their morning bulletins – a blonde woman in her mid-twenties had been burnt alive in an apparent attack. My father happened to be listening, having coffee with a friend in his carport while the radio played in the background. He had shaken his head, wondering how such a thing could happen in Perth, in Australia. He was born in Serbia and had immigrated to Australia in search of a safer life for him and his future children. This was not the sort of thing that people did to each other, even in his homeland, which had broken apart in a savage civil war a few years after he'd left. Dad and his friend talked about it for a while, wondering what had happened, and about the suffering it would cause for the poor girl and her family. He never for a moment considered that it might've been his daughter who'd been attacked.

My eldest sister, Suzie, was in Melbourne celebrating the first birthday of my nephew. Out of all the days in the world, I had to get burnt on this special occasion, my nephew's birthday. She was thousands of kilometres away from me when she finally heard the news.

Svetlana had been out driving with her husband, Filip, when she heard about the attack on the radio, and fear gripped her heart. She'd been calling me through the morning and I hadn't answered or called her back, which was out of the ordinary.

'Filip, what if that's Dana?' she asked, hearing my neighbourhood mentioned on the radio. She tried to call me and again it went through to voicemail. I always answered Svet's calls, or called her back within minutes, and when I didn't, she began to panic, urging Filip to turn the car around and drive to my apartment.

'Don't be silly, baby,' Filip had said. But Svet knew. We're the children of Eastern European immigrants, and while I don't believe in all that superstitious ooga-booga stuff from the old country, me and Svet have always shared a bond that's even closer than sisterhood. That day, some-how, she knew. She started screaming to Filip, 'Turn this car around! I have to go check!'

When their car pulled into the road leading up to my apartment building, her fears were confirmed. The street was blocked off with police tape, with forensic investiga-tors moving in and out of the building, red and blue lights flashing everywhere, and TV news crews filming reporters in front of the whole scene. Svet went wild and tried to charge through the police lines to get to me. The media turned their attention to her just in time to see her being held back by the cops. There's footage of her throwing her purse at the police, screaming, 'This is my sister's house! I'm her sister! Look at my ID, where is she?'

The only one in the family who knew exactly where I was happened to be my poor mum, Vera. She worked at Royal Perth as a patient care assistant, and she was upstairs when I was brought in. When Svetlana found out where I'd gone she called Mum, and Mum raced to intensive care. Even though nobody was supposed to be allowed in, she was able to use her hospital ID to get past security. She was the first to see me – and what she saw still gives her nightmares. I was naked and scalded pink all over. Already, I looked nothing like I had when I'd gone to sleep the previous night. Mum says that she couldn't recognise me, her own daughter, and for a moment she hoped that it was all some terrible mistake, that this wasn't her Dana lying there like a corpse, arms spread out like I'd been crucified. To this day, she can't talk about it without bursting into tears.

I don't blame her. I was messed up. My whole body above the waist was taken by the fire. I suffered burns to 64 per cent of my body, most of them full-thickness. The protein that made up my skin, muscle and flesh was denatured. This means that both layers of skin (epidermis and dermis) were completely destroyed, and much of the muscle and fat underneath was superheated beyond repair.

On most of my back, I've got no fat at all, just muscle and fascia, the tough layer of connective tissue that's meant to lie between them. And the sensory nerves in my skin were lost.

The dead skin would soon turn into a dense, white, leathery shell – called eschar – which would have to be surgically removed. I was unconscious for the first of the dozens of operations I'd require, but that doesn't diminish the horror. As my skin started to harden, what was left of my flesh was swelling like a balloon, so I was at risk of my body crushing itself with the pressure of the swelling. To stop that happening, the surgeons had to make long cuts into the burnt flesh, a procedure called an escharotomy, all along my sides, my arms, every finger. To this day, much of my body is criss-crossed with a fine lattice of scars from where scalpels sliced through me to prevent the worst of it.

The standard procedure for a burn like mine would be to wait seventy-two hours before debriding the dead flesh and replacing it with skin grafts, but in my case they had to wait another twenty-four hours after that, because it was just too risky. The damage was too extensive and the infection too severe. All they could do was keep me on life support, pumping my system with antibiotics and fluids designed to bring the infection under control.

And all my family could do was hope and pray, as they tried to come to terms with what happened and how something so evil had gripped our family.

One by one, my friends and family converged on the waiting room. At first I was in the emergency department and they couldn't get in to see me, but, after many hours, when they finally could, their hearts broke. I have photos of the first hours that even I can't stand to look at, so imagine how it was for my poor family. When Svetlana came into the room she rushed over to the bedside and fell to her knees, screaming. My dad arrived and went into a state of shock. He temporarily forgot how to speak English and started ranting in Serbian, then chanting, these long, keening religious chants. Mum, meanwhile, was inconsolable, just screaming and weeping. She and Dad embraced; it was the first time they'd seen each other in a long time. What a reunion.

On top of all this the room was full of police, who had no idea what had happened to me but were treating it as an attempted homicide. For all they knew, whoever had done this to me was going to come back and try to finish it. Uniformed cops and plain-clothed detectives were bombarding my family with questions, but wouldn't tell them anything in return, keeping all information about the crime away from them. That would become a pattern for the next eighteen months. Over that period, every moment would be full of agonising indecision and misinformation for my family. And just plain old agony for me.

I had been slender and healthy, but the physique that I'd worked so hard to maintain actually worsened my chances of survival. If I'd had more fat, it would have absorbed more of the damage that ended up being dealt to my muscles and organs. To help save what was left, I was immediately put on a complicated life-support and fluid-management program – a breathing tube down my throat and intravenous tubes snaking in and out of my body, flooding my system with vital medication, antibiotics, hydration and nutrients.

As it was, my body went into crisis mode. It started redirecting blood from other organs into the two that are the most important for survival: the brain and the heart. My heart rate doubled as my immune system raced to stop the infection crowding into my broken body. The average heart rate of a healthy woman of my age is around 60–80 beats per minute. For a burns survivor, that speeds up to as fast at 150 beats per minute. The body is frantically trying to heal, which requires huge amounts of nutrition, more than the body can possibly absorb. In particular, the amount of protein required is extraordinary. Every inch of my burnt flesh was screaming out for protein, and so the risk was that my body would start to use up its few remaining resources, ripping the protein out of the muscles that had escaped the fire.

When I had lived through the first hour, the doctors kept working and my family prayed for me to last another. The prognosis was touch and go for days. Svetlana sat in the waiting room begging for information, for hope, from the doctors. They would say things like, 'Let's see if she makes it through the next hour.' It went on for days – the doctors were very careful to give my family limited information because burns recovery is such a long, painful process.

That first night, there was no good news for my family, no relief, just updates every few hours that I was still fighting. The doctors were careful to provide only the information that my family needed to get through the current window of time. Whenever Svetlana asked for information about what my future might look like, they would say, 'We'll cross that bridge when we come to it.' They probably didn't rate my chances of survival as very high.

In cases like mine, burns surgeons have to make tough decisions, and quickly. As soon as my system could handle it the surgeons would have to debride my wounds. This meant removing the dead tissue to stave off the likely fatal infection it would cause, while saving as much of me as possible. After the skin denatures and turns white, your body recognises it as dead cells and wants to get rid of it. Left to its own devices, my body might eventually have shed that skin, but with the extent of my injuries I would never have survived until then. The surgeons had to shut the wound down by removing the dead skin and replacing it. But the more skin they took away, the worse my scarring and eventual disfigurement would be. The decisions they made in those moments would determine the rest of my life: my face, my fingers, my mobility, the extent of scarring; my independence.

In most bad burns, the surgeons will want to debride the dead skin as quickly as possible, getting the major surgery out of the way so that the body can begin healing sooner, offering the best chance of recovery and reduced scarring. But my system was too badly damaged for them to risk doing that. In the first hours everything was so badly infected they had to defer any surgery beyond what was absolutely necessary for my survival in order to deal with the swelling. The risk of me dying on the table was far too great.

In fact, I did die, technically. Despite having the finest medical care possible, on the second night my breathing stopped and my heart sputtered out. I flatlined. It took the considerable skill of the doctors and all the luck in the world (and maybe the will of God) to start my heart up again.

It took three days to stabilise me to the point where the big operations could commence. In some ways I was actually quite lucky it took so long for the surgery to become viable. My ears had been burnt to a crisp and all blood-supply to them had stopped. It looked like they were going to have to amputate them as dead, useless skin, but at the last minute the blood flow resumed and the surgeons were able to save my ears. Once again – a silver lining.

Nearly a hundred hours after the attack I was deemed fit for surgery. Still in an induced coma, my burnt skin was removed and replaced with grafts from my legs, bum – anywhere they could find unburnt flesh. The doctors decided to delay a facial graft until my immune system was in better fighting condition. Waiting until I was a little stronger to do that surgery meant those scars would be much less severe once they healed. Thank God.

Meanwhile, my family waited. Friends and extended family from far-flung corners of my life would come and sit with my mum, dad and siblings, providing what support they could until they were exhausted. Every hour the doctors would come in and report on my condition, and each time the best news they could offer was that I wasn't dead yet.

Svet had immediately taken charge. She'd always looked after me and now, in the middle of all the chaos and distress of the waiting room, she kept her cool. She had a background in psychology with a particular interest in the science of neuropsychology, so she knew enough about medicine to understand what the doctors were saying and to translate it for the rest of the family. Whenever she could, she would take aside one of the treatment team and question them about what was happening, what she could do to aid in my recovery. As friends and relatives came in all shocked and distraught, she did her best to calm them down and keep everyone strong. She kept it cool, but inside she was falling apart.

Just before I was attacked there had been a tragic series of bushfires and the Royal Perth was chock-full of people recovering from bad burns. So while my family were waiting for news of me, they were sharing the waiting room with the families of other burns victims who were fighting for their lives. And some were losing. Svetlana became friendly with the family of a man who had suffered burns less extensive than mine, and who was two and a half months into his fight for survival. Svet was with them when they found out he had succumbed, just died from the shock to his system, months after escaping the fire. Poor Svet was horrified, but couldn't tell anyone. She didn't want my mum and dad to know just how precarious my situation was; just how close I was to death. The stress of keeping up a brave face under all that horror must have been incredible. At the time she was nursing her newborn baby, my little nephew Piglet. That's not his real name, obviously, but we called him piglet because he was the hungriest baby you could ever meet, and as he got older he would continue to eat anything he could get his hands on, so the name stuck. Poor Piglet, with the stress of the situation, Svet's milk just dried up entirely. Svet was strong, but more than anyone, she knew just how bad things were.

While I was fighting for my life, the police were struggling to work out why I'd been attacked. The investigating cops quickly ruled out gangland ties, and I'd never been involved in violence in the past. They could find no motive or suspect, especially for such a vicious and brutal act of violence. Their initial suspicion was that it was an act of domestic violence, and they asked my friends and family who I was seeing. Somebody gave them poor Paul's number, the guy who'd visited me the night before the attack, and not long after that the police kicked in his door and took him in for questioning. He was quickly cleared and let go, but it can't have been easy for him.

The police were not taking any chances when it came to investigating the case. Many of them were experienced, hardened officers but they had never seen anything like this. Detective Senior Constable David Johnson, who ran the investigation, would later tell the media that it was one of the most severe and most horrendous crimes he'd ever encountered. This alone is testimony to the random, senseless nature of Natalie's rage and delusion. Her attack on me came out of nowhere, just like her hatred.

I was the only person who could tell them what happened, and with no way to be sure that I would ever wake up, given the extent of my injuries, the police asked Svetlana to make a public appeal at a press conference. She stood in front of the cameras and tearfully urged the public for help. 'Our family are living minute to minute. We can't sleep, we can't eat. If you know what happened, you have to come forward and let the police finish this.'

Almost immediately, people began calling the police with tips. The few people I'd told about the threatening phone calls were able to produce a name, which led the police to start making inquiries about Natalie. It turns out that my assailant had been running around for a month telling everyone she was going to kill me – not the smartest thing she could have done. In no time at all, the police had only one suspect.

The police began secretly recording Natalie's phone calls. Over the next few days she made many calls to her ex-husband, Edin, and her brother Dejan, in which they talked about me, speaking in Macedonian. Luckily one of the investigating officers was fluent in the language and was on to her instantly. They were listening when Natalie talked about dyeing her hair brown – just after the media had reported that the police were looking for a blonde woman in her twenties.

Then, eight days after the attack, the police intercepted a call from Natalie to her brother, in which she said she was on her way to Perth airport to flee the country.

It turns out that when Natalie and Daniel Stone had broken into my apartment to attack me they had another girl, Jessica Mazza, waiting in their car. When Natalie climbed back into the car, she'd turned to Mazza and told her not to say anything about this to anyone or she'd kill her too.

Three days after my attack, Jessica Mazza had been picked up by the police as a witness to the assault – a witness who would lead the police straight to Natalie. Just forty-five minutes after she received a phone call with the news the police were speaking to Mazza, Natalie bought a one-way ticket out of the country – and ran to the airport without any luggage, or her child. She was heading first to Istanbul, then Macedonia.

The cops raced to the airport to stop her and apprehended her just in the nick of time. If she got into the air, the chances of her getting away with the crime sky-rocketed. There was a hectic rush for the police to get units to the airport, and they got there just in time to see her arrive and dump her car. She made straight for the terminal, but it was too late. Detective Senior Constable Johnson and his team caught her on the way to the plane. He arrested her on the spot. According to the police, she looked shocked. She really thought she'd got away with it.

For a while, it looked like she would. She denied everything, denied all knowledge of the attack, or even knowing who I was – even feigning sympathy when they told her about my condition. This was eight days after the attack. I was still in an induced coma and, as far as the police knew, I was the only witness to what had really happened in my apartment. Without my testimony it would be hard for them to prove that she was the psychopath who'd turned me into a human fireball. All they could do, like my family, was pray for me to wake up.

And two days later, I did.

chapter 6

WAKING UP

I came back from death's door slowly. Two days before I regained consciousness, around the same time Natalie was being put in cuffs at Perth airport, I was starting to respond to stimuli; flinching when someone pricked me. My brother Denis was by my bedside and was the first to notice this early sign. Then my mum, who had been weeping by my side for over a week, begged me, 'Dana, can you hear me? Please show me a sign, a blink or anything.' At the time I was staring blindly at the ceiling, but then, just like that, a blink. It was enough to give my family hope. But I wasn't out of the woods yet, not by a long shot.

My whole family had been staying by my bedside the whole time. As far as they all knew, I was never coming back. But, just in case I could hear her, they talked to me about what was happening; told me that they were sure that I would make it, that they had no idea who had done this to me, nobody did, even the police were baffled. Svetlana spoke to me about memories from our childhood, stories that we'd reminisced over before. Remember this time? Remember that time?

While I slept, I dreamt. Snatches of memory, fantasy, nightmare. These dreams faded in and out, but Svetlana was in some of them. Sometimes it was just the impression of her, a feeling, maybe her voice or a snatch of song that reached me in the coma.

She would sing to me while I was in the coma – pop tunes, songs from our childhood. Songs we used to sing together and dumb little tunes from our favourite TV shows or Disney movies.

She was singing the Whitney Houston song 'Step by Step', which we'd loved and sang together growing up, when I finally woke up.

I began to softly mouth the words with her, before I croaked, 'Svet,' my voice just a whisper, ruined by the tubes down my throat and the smoke and flames that had engulfed me.

'Dana?' Svetlana sat bolt upright and took my hand.

'Shut up, Svet,' I whispered. 'You can't sing for shit.'

Svetlana broke into happy tears. Underneath the burns, I was still the same cheeky Dana.

I always think about how ironic it was that I woke up to that particular song, as if I already knew the step-by-step battle that lay ahead of me.

That first day, when I woke up, the police were waiting. They were the first people I spoke to, before the rest of my family even had a chance to really say hello. One minute I'd woken up with Svet and my family by my side, the next, detectives were ordering everyone out of the room and sitting down to question me. The whole time I'd been fighting for my life, they'd been investigating the attack. They had a lot of questions they wanted answered. They set up a video camera and began to question me.

'We just need to know what happened,' they said before switching on the camera. 'Tell us everything you remember.'

I was in no state to be giving evidence, but the police didn't seem to mind. To be honest, I didn't really know what was going on. This was only ten days after the attack and I was physically broken, and messed up from the cocktail of drugs that had been put together to keep me alive and away from the worst of the pain.

Later on, this would cause all sorts of problems for me, but at the time I wanted to give the police as much information as I could. I didn't know that they had Natalie in custody or how much evidence they had against her. They mainly wanted to know why I was attacked, which is a question I still don't have a clear answer for. I guess the police were worried that Natalie's crime was not an isolated incident – that there was more violence to come. I told them what I could. After they finished interviewing me they packed up their camera and left, and I passed out again.

In the following weeks I would drift in and out of consciousness, dreaming of being whole again, of an end to the pain, and then come to, unable to understand what had happened to me. Reality and fantasy merged into one horrifying twilight world. I was having the most vividly real yet wild dreams.

People often ask me if I have nightmares about the night I was burnt. They think that I must have a phobia of fire. That, once you've been burnt alive, every time you close your eyes, all you can see is flames. But I've never had one nightmare about it. Not one. Not about the attack itself or the events of the night. But I did have another nightmare, one terrible dream that recurred over and over again for the first six months in that windowless hospital room.

In this dream, I would be wearing a pink dress, a beautiful mini. And I would be wearing it at a club, somewhere really fancy – always the same club, always the same dream.

I would be standing at the top of winding gold stairs and looking down at a huge room that was all marble, with gold tables, and people here and there, but not too many. The sort of place I would have really loved to go to before the burn. In the dream I would walk down the stairs and on the way I would pass a mirror. I would check myself out and find that I looked like I did before the burn. I was really calm and at peace and happy with the way I looked – smooth skin, head held high.

Then I would wake up in my hospital bed, paralysed and restrained by compression bandages, crying my eyes out.

Honestly, that dream felt so real, and then each time I'd have to face reality – reality was the real nightmare, and there was no waking up from it. Then I'd cry, and cry, and cry, because I'd have to face the terrible day ahead. In the blur of agonising wound dressings, painful physio, the looks of pity and the strong drugs, it was hard to stay focused. From the very first day, the suffering was unbelievable.

Apart from the recurring dream of the pink dress, I would drift off into flashbacks from childhood that felt so real I could have practically been there. Then suddenly I'd veer off into the most bizarre psychedelic situations. I would be flying through the sky, but in a world filled entirely with shoes – Louboutin, Valentino, Jimmy Choo, Yves Saint Laurent. I'd just be zooming through all these flying shoes, having the time of my life, and then suddenly I'd be in a nightclub, ordering tequila shots. Then back to childhood, playing on the beach on Koolan Island. Then waking up in the ICU.

At first, I was too heavily drugged to really understand the situation. I was convinced that the nurses looking after me were keeping me there against my will. That they were part of a conspiracy to torture me. Svet would sit by my bedside and I would beg her to help me escape from the hospital. She would patiently explain that she couldn't do that, not right now. She is beyond angelic, my sister.

The things she has done for me, the patience and grace of that woman.

For example: for the first few days after I was conscious, all I wanted was water, but my body wouldn't have been able to handle it. Part of intensive care meant strict fluid management. Svet told me later that I had 72 litres of fluid IVed into me and dozens of litres of blood – she said I was like jelly, with my body unable to hold any fluids in. The tubes threading in and out of my body were slowly rehydrating me, and that's all I could hope for.

'Please,' I would beg every time a nurse came to change a drip over. 'Please give me some water. Just a sip.' They all shook their heads sadly.

There was one nurse who would sometimes take pity on me and dip a cotton bud in water for me to suck on. You'd better believe I treasured it, sucked on it like a baby given her first ever lollipop.

The rest of the time, I just couldn't understand why they wouldn't help me; I was too out of it on painkillers.

One time I dreamt that I got up from my hospital bed, picked up my handbag, strolled down to the hospital cafeteria, bought not one but *nineteen* cold drinks, came back upstairs, put the drink into a mini fridge that I thought was next to my bed, and went to sleep. When I woke up, Svetlana was holding my hand.

'Svet,' I croaked. 'Can you get my drink?'

'Dana, sis,' she said gently, 'you don't have a drink. You can't yet. Soon.'

This made me unspeakably angry. 'Don't lie to me, Svet! I just bought it with my own money! Are you lying to me? Are you working with them?'

'Who is "them"?' Svet had asked, patiently.

'The nurses. You're working with them!'

Svet just patiently explained that I was mistaken, that I couldn't have walked to go get a drink – because I couldn't walk. But I wasn't having it.

'Bullshit, Svet. I just paid $80 for drinks! They're all right there in the fridge.'

'Dana, love, there is no fridge.'

'It's right there!' I yelled.

I pointed to where the fridge had been in my dream and saw that Svet was right, that there was nothing there. I had no drink, and couldn't go get one because I couldn't walk.

My eyes filled with tears as I realised she was right. I couldn't even have held a drink if Svet had handed me one. Every time I had one of these hallucinations, and my mind cleared and I came back to reality, the gravity of my situation would bring me crashing down and I would weep.

Those sorts of hallucinations happened every day and I was always confused and angry in the middle of them. One thing that didn't change in me was the wide and crude vocabulary I had at my disposal. Ask anyone who knew me before the attack – I'd never been shy about expressing myself. Hovering at death's door didn't change that. If I thought someone was doing me wrong, I would fight back, but with my limited grasp on reality that made for some unfortunate misunderstandings.

I remember suddenly becoming aware that I was bald. My hair, eyebrows and eyelashes had all been burnt off. I was as smooth as a newborn baby, but I couldn't remember why. In my diminished state, I was sure someone had shaved my head in my sleep. I lay there fuming.

The second a nurse walked by I went pyscho at her. 'Hey, lady! Why the fuck did you shave my head?'

Try as she might, the poor woman couldn't convince me that she hadn't snuck in and shaved my head as a joke. I was like that with all sorts of things until they finally eased up on the medication.

Slowly I returned to reality, but that wasn't a good thing. As painful and scary as being set on fire is, the aftermath is a million times worse – because with it came the understanding of just how damaged my poor body was. I had full-thickness burns to over half of my body and to my face, which meant the skin and much of what was underneath it was gone. The muscle and fat on my front had survived better than that on my back. When I'd stopped, dropped and rolled, I'd lost pretty much everything from my shoulderblades down to my hips.

To cover the gaping wounds where the burnt flesh had been removed, the surgeons skimmed skin off my legs, scalp, bum – anywhere they could – and prepared it for skin grafts. It's a complex procedure, but basically they take the cut section of skin and stretch it out with a mesher, a machine that expands it to four times its original size. This means that small amounts of skin can be used to cover larger areas. It's a medical miracle, but it gives the skin a kind of a weird, dimpled look, kind of like flyscreen mesh.

I ended up wearing my scalp on my face, my groin on my neck, my hips in my armpits; I was put back together like a human jigsaw puzzle. The only parts of my face where I still have my original skin are the lines around my mouth and small parts of my eyelids. Those are the only inches of skin that didn't get burnt – I think that's because I was screaming at the time and using my hands to shield my eyes. The rest of me is put together from whatever they could save. Honestly, I'm like modern-day Frankenstein – which is kind of cool!

It was a while until I knew that, though. Even after I'd stabilised and become lucid, the doctors were careful with how much information they gave me. When they thought I was ready they told me that the muscle might regenerate, but that the fat I had lost would never grow back in certain places. For the rest of my life, it would just be skin and bone, pretty much.

The fine muscles in my hands were almost destroyed. They told me that I would probably never even be able to hold a pencil again.

Luckily, everything below the waist was saved from the flames so, in time, I could learn to walk again – but for now I was helpless.

Time passed slowly in the ICU. I had nothing to do, nothing to distract me. I was stretched out on a raised bed that kept my arms and legs restrained, to stop them contracting back into my body as the skin grafts took and the scars expanded. For endless hours I would stare at the ceiling with nothing to occupy me except my thoughts. Visits were strictly family-only and they would wait hours and hours for a ten-minute visit. They were restricted to only two people at a time and they had to be gowned, masked and gloved for quarantine reasons. My room was a hermetically sealed chamber behind two airlocks. My immune system was still ultra-vulnerable to infection. If somebody had come in with the common cold virus on their hands and touched me, it could have killed me.

So instead, I waited. I dreamt. My family put photos on the wall of my room, of Mum, Dad, my sisters, my brother, my dog. I asked for extra photos of Killer. God I missed him, my poor little dog. Last time he saw me I was burning to death on the floor of my apartment. I used to beg the medical team to let Killer in to visit me, but there was no chance. For my recovery the environment needed to be completely sterile, and Killer was . . . not that.

Sometimes my mind wandered to places I'd have preferred it didn't go, when I was in a really dark place and thinking about why I was in the hospital in the first place. During these moments, when I closed my eyes I could see Natalie's face, hear her laughing at me while she left me to die. I thought about how she could've been the last face

I'd seen on this earth. I thought of everything she'd taken away from me.

Those were really the only occasions I thought about the attack, though, or about my attackers. I'd made a decision very early on that I didn't want to let her have another second of my time or attention. It seemed to me that to do so was to give her too much credit, would have been letting her win. And I wasn't about to let evil win. But there were times, in those moments when I felt really low – true despair – when I couldn't help it and my thoughts would turn to her. Thankfully, those moments were few and far between, but when they did come, they were severe.

After a month in intensive care, the doctors judged that I was healthy enough to move to the burns ward. There I would start a new regime of treatments and painful physiotherapy; a blur of agony, looks of pity, and drugs so strong it was hard to stay focused as my limbs were manipulated and wounds were dressed and redressed.

Up until then, I'd had a team of physios moving me three times every day – a pretty limited sort of emergency physiotherapy in bed. Even though I couldn't move, every few hours physios and nurses would come in and move my arms, legs and fingers to keep them active and alive until I had healed enough to move them on my own. They'd been doing that even when I was still in the coma. Now, on the ward, I was going to be responsible for my own physio.

'It's going to hurt,' one nurse warned me. 'It's not a lot of fun, but it's so important.'

'I can't wait,' I told them.

I couldn't wait. I could handle pain, I thought. And it meant getting out of the claustrophobic little ICU room, which felt more like a prison cell. I would be able to see my loved ones again; all my family, of course, but also my friends.

At the time I was attacked, my oldest friend Jackie was living in Europe. I hadn't seen her in two years. When she heard the news she'd flown home, and now she could finally come and see me. One of my best friends, Stella, flew in as well, and my sister Suzie came over from Melbourne. Despite everything I was going through, I felt so lucky to have such awesome friends and family by my side.

I only found this out years later, but before she'd come in, Svet had taken Jackie aside and briefed her.

'It's scary, what's happened, but you need to be strong. You can't look upset. You need to be there for Dana and we need to keep her spirits up. Don't tell her anything that will break her heart.'

When Jackie came in she did her best to look nonchalant, like she was happy to see me and nothing else was wrong – but I'd known this woman my whole life and I could tell she was horrified by what she saw.

'Hi Danché,' she said, using her nickname for me from our childhood. 'How are you doing?'

'Look at me!' I burst into tears, I couldn't help it. 'Look what's happened to me!'

I could see Jackie being torn apart inside. How on one hand she wanted to rush over and comfort me, but on the other knew she had to hold back. She could tell I wanted validation from someone I'd known forever, and she wasn't going to break my heart. So, instead, she cracked a joke.

'Look, Danché,' she said, 'you're right, I'm not loving this new haircut.'

I loved her for trying to make me laugh, but I still wanted to know what she saw when she looked at me. At that point, I hadn't been allowed anywhere near a mirror, and the curiosity was driving me mad.

Burns survivors whose faces have been badly damaged often talk about the moment when they see their new face as the hardest part – but for me, that wasn't actually so bad. The day it happened, I was being taken for a shower by the nurses, not long after I'd been transferred from ICU. On the way, I asked them to stop and show me what I looked like in the mirror. They weren't into the idea at first, but I was pretty convincing, and eventually they agreed.

What I saw didn't break my heart, as I was scared it might. I looked different, sure, and I had some minor scarring from the grafts, but the swelling had gone down and my skin was already starting to smooth out. Apart from that, it really wasn't too bad. I thought that maybe it looked like I'd been really ill, like I was in the middle of a battle with cancer, and that once I grew back my hair and eyebrows I would look pretty much like I used to.

I was blissfully ignorant of what would come next.

chapter 7

SCAR TISSUE

As the initial shock of the burns and skin transplants began to settle down, I began to think that maybe things weren't so bad. My only real knowledge of burns and recovery came from movies, and from high-profile cases in the media. When I looked in the mirror, the person who was staring back didn't seem that badly injured. I looked nothing like the survivors you see on TV from time to time – their faces all crisscrossed with scar tissue. My doctors had been brilliant, had performed miracles on me. They saved my hands, my fingers, my nose, my eyes and ears. I began to think that I was going to be okay, that I would be that one miracle case, that I would be spared the agony of losing everything that had defined me.

I'd always been so proud of my skin. My mixed Serbian and Macedonian heritage had gifted me with a

Mediterranean glow. I never wore fake tan because I was lucky enough to have a body that tanned really gently and naturally in the Perth sunshine. I rarely even had to wear sunscreen unless I was spending the whole day at the beach. But now there would be no more glorious sunshiny days like that for me.

Through the first three months, the scars were bad, but they would get much worse. Scars have a period of maturation, which can last years. In this period they will grow larger, and angrier, and tighter. In bad burns, the scarring becomes so intense it can quickly disable you completely.

Luckily I had Svet there to help me research medical options from day dot, and to help me contact people all over the world about burn treatments. You'd better believe that the minute I was well enough to work my iPhone, using a special pointer, I would stay up late into the night in my hospital bed, researching and reading everything I could find on burns and scars. I read until my eyes felt as though they were bleeding, looking for hope, for any kind of information, and there was almost nothing out there. The one question I really needed answered – how bad was it going to get? – was met with deafening silence. I simply didn't know what my future would look like – if I had one. Night after night I would seek out someone who'd been through what I was going through, something that would give me that tiny glimmer of hope that I so desperately needed at that point in my life. Night after night,

I turned up nothing. The inspiration I was hoping for was just not out there.

Scars are so deceptive. They mislead you into thinking everything is going to be okay. A month after the burn I thought I was going to just be a woman with some gnarly scars and a story to tell. A year later, I ended up with scars worse than I could have possibly imagined. A year after that, they were even worse. Imagine what it's like to wake up every day and limp to the mirror, knowing even before you get there that your scars had worsened in the night. The scars started to overlap and push against each other, forming ridges and craters in my skin. By the time the scars stopped getting worse it looked like I was getting my makeup tips from Freddy Krueger. Honestly, I had more craters than the moon. I would look up at the night sky and be jealous of that bitch's skin.

The way the scars affected my looks hurt, but that wasn't even the worst problem. As they grew larger and harder, they began to restrict my mobility, as parts of my body began to lock up under the contracting tissue. The first to go were my arms. They were terribly burnt and all the muscle inside them was wasted away, so I couldn't fight the scarring. Before long they were locked up in front of me like little claws.

I couldn't do anything – dress myself, brush my teeth, any of it. The nurses on the burns ward had to do it all for me. It was heartbreaking to be so helpless, to go from being an independent young woman in the prime of my life to being a total invalid. I'd always been a very friendly and open person, and I loved the company of strangers, but it was no fun to have to interrupt a new nurse as she walked by the bed: 'Excuse me, I'm terribly sorry to bother you, I don't mean to be rude, but could you please wipe my arse?'

There was one day I tried to do it for myself, but it didn't end well. I'd just gone the toilet, then went back in to my room and started chatting to a nurse I was friendly with. Everyone kind of laughed uneasily, and then my friend the nurse pointed down at my private area.

'Um . . . Dana?'

I looked down, and saw that I had a massive piece of toilet paper stuck to me, just dangling there. I couldn't even reach down to remove it. It was so embarrassing, all I could do was burst out laughing. I laughed so hard that I almost wet myself (but that would have been fine, because I already had toilet paper handy).

Even though the staff on the ward were all amazing, they couldn't be everywhere at once. A lot of times, especially at night, when something was wrong, or I needed help to swallow a sip of water or to get up and go to the toilet, I would just have to wait until help became available.

I peed myself so many times that night, with my urine burning the wounds on my legs. I felt so helpless. I was screaming for help but nobody could hear me since I had lost my voice and the room was air compression-restricted.

Because Mum worked in another part of the hospital she had a security pass that let her into the burns ward, so she was able to come and see me outside of regular visiting hours, thank God. If it wasn't for her turning up at all hours of the day and night to help me I wouldn't have made it through the first few months. One time she turned up at 5 a.m. and found me crying in my bed. I'd needed to go to the toilet all night, but the buzzer to summon the nurse was out of my reach. All I could do was lie in the dark in pain and hope that somebody came by. Nobody did.

I was so helpless, calling out desperately, but nobody could hear me with my broken voice too weak to penetrate the air-sealed room. Help didn't come for hours, until Mum came in and called a nurse for me.

The nurses and ward staff did their best, but they were only human. My family, on the other hand, were superhuman. From the very first days, my mum and sisters had to become my full-time caregivers. Svet, especially, did everything for me. She gave up her whole life pretty much, just to look after me, and didn't ask anything in return.

Well, except for one thing: she asked me to fight and never give up. In return, she promised she would never stop helping me – and she never has.

Svet's still my big sister, though, and just because I was in the hospital didn't mean she would stop teasing me. She used to mess with my hair. It all burnt off in the fire, and it went through this stage where it regrew as a really unflattering mullet. I begged Svet to fix it for me. So she was like, 'Sure, Dana. I'll make you real pretty,' and went and got her hairdressing gear. And then she went in and really styled that mullet up until I was full MacGyver!

When it finally grew long enough that she could do something more with it, she offered to style me up properly. She got a brush and a hairdryer and started fussing with my hair. It was a really big moment for us – full of sisterly love, with us bonding while she fussed with my locks. I was eternally grateful for her helping me regain my dignity and femininity.

So she was doing my hair like a proper hairdresser, chatting away, and then, out of nowhere, she started reminiscing about our childhood, about the toys that were in fashion when we were kids. Cabbage Patch Kids, Tamagotchis, those little Troll Dolls with the big hair that were big in the '90s. She kept talking about the trolls and I couldn't figure out why – until she finished doing my hair and brought the mirror over.

She'd full-on sabotaged me! She'd blow-dried my hair up to look exactly like a Troll Doll. I was furious, but she was just pissing herself laughing. I roared at her, waving my little T-rex arms in her direction, until finally I started laughing too. She could always make me laugh, no matter what, which is exactly what I needed at that point.

Believe, me, there wasn't much in life to laugh about. My scars were some of the worst the burns team had seen before. Compared to other patients with similar injuries my skin responded by producing particularly aggressive scars, and my tissue got red and raised very quickly. It's almost impossible to do anything about it.

Professor Suzanne Rea, even with all her experience, was dismayed by how bad my scars were.

'You have a very florid scar response,' she explained to me gently one day. 'We don't really know why but, as your body is healing, the scars are particularly aggressive and pronounced.'

As they grew, they would raise off my skin, sometimes up to 2 centimetres off the plane of my face and body. As they rose, the skin would tighten and be pulled in strange directions. It wasn't soft or pliable at all – it was like tough leather. And when your skin turns to leather, there are consequences.

As all the skin tightens, the centre of the body starts to pull the limbs inward. It's a really weird process. Imagine that you're holding a big rubber band in your hands, long and elastic enough for you to stretch it out as far as your arms can reach. That was how my skin worked before the scarring. Now, imagine that rubber band is an inch shorter. And another inch. It's already impossible to stretch your arms all the way while holding it. Now imagine that that rubber band is shrinking every day, becoming less and less elastic. That's a little bit of what it's like, only instead of one rubber band, it's a dozen of them, restricting your movement in every direction as different plates of scar tissue begin to form.

It's bad, and it's fast; if it's not checked and treated every step of the way you will shrivel into a ball of hardened flesh. If you look at photographs of burns survivors in the developing world, many of them look like their chins have melted into their necks, their arms into their sides. It isn't the fire that does that to you, it's the healing process. And it was starting to happen to me.

I was doing occupational therapy every day with my wonderful occupational therapist, Rosemary Kendell, to try to stop the retraction process. I have so much respect and admiration for Rosemary for the work she did with me, I owe her so much. Even in the small amounts of time my family were allowed to see me, our work didn't stop. The doctors had taken everyone who visited me aside and showed them how to help me with my recovery exercises. They could help me, but they were never allowed to actually do something for me if there was a remote chance that I could do it myself. If I wanted a cup from the dresser, for example, Svet could be there to catch me if I fell, but she couldn't give it to me. I had to develop my independence from scratch, and it would take tough love to do that.

The doctors had been impressed with Svet from day one. She'd handled everything in the emergency ward, and then the ICU, with perfect calm – liaising with the doctors, translating for the family, sorting out logistics and plans for the future. And so, more than anyone else, she was entrusted with my recovery. They taught her the essential physiotherapy I would need to perform in hospital and once I was released. She was there to support me but, more than that, to push me any time I needed that little bit more hope.

In the early days, one of the things she had to really push me on was exercising my face. If I didn't move it in certain ways, the risk of scars locking my whole face up was very real. There was a big medical chart behind my bed with all the facial expressions I had to force myself to practise, and all these sounds I needed to make to stop my mouth from closing over: 'Ahhhhh. Eeeeew. Oooooh.'

When Svet came in to visit, I would beg her for news, but she would be firm.

'What's up, Svet? How are my nephews? How's Mum?'

'Dana. You have to do your exercises. Repeat after me . . . ahhh, eeeew, ooooh.'

It was really painful for both of us. I could tell treating me like this was killing her, but it was saving my life. She had to be cruel to be kind.

The scars kept growing and soon they started taking over my face. My mouth started to shrink and kept getting smaller, until it was about the size of a ten-cent coin. It looked like a cat's bumhole, and the pressure deformed my jaw to the point where it started crushing my teeth. Before long the movement of my jaw was so restricted that I couldn't close my mouth. Every night the doctors would strap me into scaffolding, this sort of padded crucifix, that was designed to slow the retraction as the scar tissue took over my body.

It was a losing battle. Soon my mobility started to fade and the scars grew more aggressive. Despite everyone's tireless work with me, and me sleeping with an uncomfortable splint in my mouth to prevent retraction, my mouth started to close over. Soon it was the size of a five-cent coin. I could barely move my mouth at all, not to chew food, not to smile. My arms and body continued to stiffen and lock, and still the physiotherapy went on, hands all over me every day, poking and prodding. And all the time, the skin fused a little tighter. I felt trapped in my own body.

My entire body was swaddled in compression bandages, wrapped up like a mummy. The only part of me that I'd seen in months was my face, and that looked worse every time I saw it. I began to suspect that everyone around me was conspiring to protect me from the truth. In my heart I still believed that I would be that one miracle case that managed to recover quickly and flawlessly, to bounce back to who I had been. But at that point I realised that people were carefully drip-feeding me information, swaddling me in hope just as tightly as with the bandages, to protect me from reality until my mind was strong enough to take it.

I was really upset. I already couldn't believe that my skin, something I literally couldn't live without, could be so badly damaged. It got to the point where one day, during a clinic with Suzanne Rea and Fiona Wood, I demanded to know what would happen to me.

'Tell me the truth, please,' I begged them. 'What are my chances?'

And Professor Rea gave it to me – the truth – as gently as she could. 'Your scars are going to get significantly worse than they are right now. Don't ever expect to look like Dana again.' She was just being straight with me, but it was a hard thing to hear. I couldn't really believe it, not at first. I had to see it for myself.

Soon after that, when my mum and Svetlana were visiting, I asked them to take a photo of my back. They exchanged a look, full of sadness and worry, and that look filled me with dread.

'Take a photo of my back,' I demanded.

'No, darling,' said Mum. 'You don't want to see.'

Yes, I did want to see. 'Take a photo of my back!' I yelled.

Mum and Svet looked at each other again, and Svet nodded. She moved behind me and snapped a photo on her phone, then came up to me and showed me.

The doctors had told me that the damage to my back was serious and irreparable, but that had only been an idea, a kind of abstract thought, until I saw it with my own eyes. What had once been a smooth expanse of golden skin between my neck and the bottom of my hips was now a mess of scar tissue. Raised scars ran along craters in the flesh where my fat cells had been destroyed. And in my hip, there was a huge, gaping open wound through which I could see right into my body. I'd never seen anything so horrific before, on the ward or in the most nightmarish horror film. When Svet showed me what I'd become, I was hanging on to the bed and just wanted to get away. I collapsed and fell, emotionally broken into tiny pieces on the hospital floor. That was it. Every bit of my soul, every fibre of my being, lost all hope. That was the first time I believed that I wasn't Dana any more. I was broken, a gone person.

I was beginning to comprehend just how much had been taken from me. I didn't just lose my looks the day of the attack; I lost my entire life, my ability of function, my independence, my sexuality – every single thing that was a physical element of my identity was gone. My body was broken, but beyond that all my dreams for the future were leaking away. The moment I really understood that, when it sunk in, my soul cracked. I could feel it disappearing, all the dreams I'd had for my life, all that I wanted to do – work, travel, maybe marriage, possibly having children. I felt like none of that could be mine.

Instead I felt a cold, resolute sadness, and the realisation that I was never going to be the same. It was such a pivotal moment. I remember it so vividly, as if it's always just happened. That moment of clarity that I was well and truly fucked.

There's a photo I have that I think captures where I was emotionally at that time. It's hard for me to see, even today. I can go back and look at photos from any stage of my recovery and take them as they are. Photos from day one, looking like a corpse? No problem. Photos from the debridement operations where they are stripping back my skin and you can see all the delicate muscles and veins of my back? Doesn't really bother me. But that one photo still brings tears to my eyes.

It was taken only a few months into my recovery, the first time I'd seen my little nephew since the attack. He'd been born just a few weeks before my burn, and the minute I was well enough for him to come into the hospital, Svet brought him in to see me – there's a photograph of the exact moment.

I'm sitting in bed in my compression garments, with my little nephew, who's only months old, leaning on me, as I couldn't physically hold him. I just look broken. Completely defeated. I'm looking down at this sweet little baby and all I want to do is touch him, and I can't even do that. My hands are stiff and useless, closed up in compression bandages. In my eyes you can see the sorrow of the realisation that the attack might have taken away the thing I've always wanted more than anything else in this life: to be there for my family. In any other photo, no matter how intense it might look, no matter how badly I'm doing, there's a spark in my eyes, an irrepressible kind of liveliness. I call it my Dana energy. The photos taken of me that day – that spark is gone. I felt like I wasn't Dana anymore. I just could not fathom why the world was throwing me so much hardship and sorrow.

This moment was taken away from me, this moment of holding my little nephew. And, right then and there, I decided I wasn't going to let my attackers take anything more away from me. As fast as the light went out, it came back on again – and it was brighter than ever. I wanted to be able to hold my nephew, to touch his face. I wanted my life back. Now I just had to find a way to seize it.

chapter 8

REHAB

Surviving a burn takes work. Hard work, and more grit than you could ever imagine. You see yourself pushed to your limits, and then you crawl past them, just to maintain your humanity. It ruins your body, plays havoc with your mind. There's no sensation quite as distressing as looking in the mirror and having trouble recognising yourself as a human being.

The team at Royal Perth tried to get me moving from the day I woke up. But I was in agony, the worst pain imaginable, and getting up and doing exercise was simply not on my agenda.

I don't mean to boast, but I'm the proud owner of the filthiest vocabulary you're going to hear anywhere other than a pirate ship. Not that I use it very often – there's a time and place for everything – but then again, sometimes only a curse word will do. Such as when they tried to get me to participate in physiotherapy, particularly in those first weeks when I was still really out of it on painkillers, and my vulgar vocab had no filters, I let them have it with both barrels. Then I reloaded and let them have it again. It was clear that they were going to need a physiotherapist with superhuman levels of compassion, patience and empathy. That's when they brought in Dale.

Dale Edgar is a senior physiotherapist and researcher with two decades of specialist experience in burns and acute trauma. He's the physio who teaches other physios the best methods for treating burns survivors and improving their quality of life. He's also the most patient, kind man you could ever meet. Still, with me he had his work cut out for him. During our first session, I let him know just how much I hated it, and he kept going, calm and professional.

'Dana,' he said to me gently on that first day, 'do you really think nobody has ever told me to go fuck myself before?' He is a legend, and won me over straight away.

He took one look at me and realised how serious my injuries were, how epic my struggle was going to be. I was in a race against time, trying to build up enough muscle to regain my movement before I was locked down by scar tissue. It's a catch-22. If you don't exercise every day, you stiffen up, but at the same time my muscles were so weakened and damaged by the fire that the strength I needed to do those exercises had deserted me.

If I didn't beat the scars in those first weeks, though, then I never would. Dale tried to communicate this to me about a month after I'd moved to the ward.

'With your injuries, you've got a very limited window in which to get moving. There'll be about six weeks or so before your scars start to ramp up, and if you don't start fighting now to get your full range of movement, you're going to end up losing it all.'

Dale explained why my injuries were especially bad, and that I was going to be facing challenges that few other people had faced – and that only I could beat them. My burns were 360-degree circumferential burns, meaning they surrounded my entire torso. As my scars matured they were only going to grow tighter and tighter. Every day I was shocked anew by how much the scars affected my whole body. For instance, I've got two long scars down my sides, but they affect the skin all the way to my fingertips. If I twist my left shoulder, it pulls on scar tissue on my lower back.

The most serious problem was with my armpits. They were burnt and had been grafted, and that skin is particularly delicate, so the potential for scarring was huge. The huge grafts across my shoulder and the top of my back meant that soon two large plates of scarring would rise, impacting my movement in three directions, pushing down on my shoulders and arms, locking them in place. Dale immediately identified this as a serious issue, particularly since I was so weak. The human body only has one small muscle in charge of controlling that area, and that muscle had been destroyed. In other areas of my body I had bigger muscles, in better shape, that could have helped to push through the scar tissue and stretch it as it developed. But in this area it was a perfect storm: a huge stretch of scarring and diminished muscle power to beat it.

At first it was impossible. The pain was unbelievable, almost indescribable. I could feel it even through the heavy regime of painkillers they had given me in an ineffectual effort to numb things. Getting out of bed to balance on a medical ball was not an option.

Dale's biggest challenge as a physio was getting me to appreciate that, if I didn't get moving, I was going to be crippled. That's not something I was willing to listen to at first. He would pick me up and try to get me walking and I would just cut sick, swearing like a sailor.

We spent a hell of a lot of time together, me and Dale. Every day was a battle: me against the scars, him against me. I used to go off at him all the time. I remember one day in particular, early on, when I was learning how to walk again. I had done a couple of steps, which was all I could manage at the time – and that was with Dale basically carrying me, my legs like jelly, my feet barely touching the floor. And then he surprised me.

'Okay, Dana, we're going to cross the room, all the way to the other side.'

'No, Dale, I don't want to,' I complained, like a child.

'Come on, you have to try,' he said gently. 'If you can do it once then you can do it again.' He was always so calm and patient and logical in what he said. I'd be angry and in pain, and then suddenly I'd realise, 'Oh, he's making sense.'

So I listened to him and really pushed myself and made it to the other side of the room. I had just reached it and was so proud of myself when he said, calm as anything, 'Okay, great! Well done. Now we have to walk back.'

I was furious! 'You fuck. You told me I just had to walk across the room and I did it!'

'And now you know you can walk back,' he said.

He didn't back down or lose his cool. I got it together and walked back across the room. When I got to the other end, he was like, 'See? See how strong you are? See what you're capable of?' And through his eyes, I was able to see what an achievement that little walk really was, that I should be proud of it – to be proud of every little victory.

That was Dale's special talent. He has an almost magical ability to really get through to his patients, to find exactly what they need to be told to push through and move towards getting better. No matter how stubborn or crass or angry I was, he would match it with patience and kindness. He knew when I'd reached my limits but, most importantly, he knew just what I could achieve if I worked for it.

Dale always made me laugh, even through the pain. At one point, while I was wrapped in my pressure garments,

I had all these open wounds that just wouldn't close. To give them a chance they put slits in the elbows of my garments. So all this pinched up elbow skin was hanging out that, given my scars, looked exactly like an old man's testicle. It became a running joke between us; Dale would come in, check me out, and ask how it was going. 'Any trouble with the testicle today? How are your testicles after the latest surgery?' Dale knew how to have a laugh, which was so important for me at the time.

He put me through hell, though, in the beginning. 'You've got to expect pain,' Dale told me. 'This is going to hurt. This is a marathon. On any given day, you're going to want to just go back to bed, but if you do that, you won't be ready to face the real trial. In five months' time, when the scars are at their strongest, you need to beat them. And you need to train for that now.'

I didn't really understand the metaphor of the marathon until I'd almost lost it. One weekend, I gave up, just for the day. Dale was out of town and the weekend physios were having a hard time trying to get me to do my exercises. I just couldn't bring myself to do it. I felt so sad, hopeless at the thought of another day of pointless, painful physical labour for seemingly no reward. The pain was too much, endless. I just needed a day off, to be left alone. I told the physios to fuck off and went back to bed.

When Dale came back on Monday and we started going through the motions, he found that over the weekend I'd stiffened up so much I was basically crippled.

Over the weekend, I'd lost the ability to do the exercises that forty-eight hours ago I'd been perfectly capable of. With a whole lot of pain and blood and f-bombs, sure, but it had been possible. Now, it just wasn't. Dale was worried. He, Fiona Wood and Suzanne Rea were all brought in to test the scar. They found that I'd lost 9 centimetres of movement range. Nine centimetres. I'd lost a third of my movement more or less overnight.

These people, the heads of my medical team, actually gasped when they realised what had happened. That was a terrifying moment. These were people at the top level of professionalism, who are so calm and together, so used to seeing trauma and horror every day without losing composure. But when they saw what a weekend in bed had done to me, they reacted with pure shock. Pretty much overnight, my neck had disappeared – the pull of the scar tissue on my chest had pulled my chin down and fused it to my neck.

My arms were frozen and locked down below my shoulders, useless as chicken wings. It had taken just one weekend of giving up the fight for the scar to grow so much that it crippled me. Once I'd lost that mobility, everything went out of whack. Try raising your arm above your head – feel all the little muscles in your back and shoulder moving in sympathy? All that was lost. No amount of swearing, ranting or raving could turn this around, no matter hard we pushed; that movement was gone. It would be a year before I could even touch my face again.

I could tell Dale was very disappointed with how much movement I'd lost over the weekend. He said to me, 'Well, that's that. You're not going to be able to dress yourself, you're not going to be able to wipe your arse, because you didn't beat the scar. Because you didn't give enough of a shit to fight.'

In terms of hard lessons, it doesn't get much more real than that. It was a wake-up call. If I didn't use it, I really would lose it. I made a decision right then to go above and beyond the minimum. I didn't want to survive – I wanted to thrive.

I would beat this burn. This burn would be my bitch.

From then on, instead of running from the pain, I learnt to appreciate it. It meant that I was still alive, that I was getting better. I began to volunteer for any procedure, any possibility of improvement, no matter how much it hurt. In time I started to develop a reputation on the ward as a masochist, because I would do things without anaesthetic or pain relief. Instead of going into theatre, I'd beg the doctors, 'Let's just do it here. Go ahead, I can take it.'

I went from complaining whenever Dale asked more of me to begging him to go harder. 'You gotta push me, you gotta snap me. Go ahead and break me. *I can take it*.' And those times he helped me to really push it through. Together we've split my arm a thousand times, and there's been cracked scar tissue and blood everywhere, and he's just been really calm, like, 'It's fine, it's fine, that's good!' And of course it wasn't really fine, but that's how he made me feel. Like I could do anything. Like I could *win*.

I'd learnt that I wasn't going to recover unless I went at it like a crazy person. It was a crazy situation and I'd have to work like crazy to beat it. What the hospital and the doctors gave me was just a start – the rest was up to me. After fucking up once and losing so much, I would never do it again.

Every day I fought to try and get back a little more of my movement and independence, and every day the scars grew stronger. I was physically broken, my movement at an all-time low, but now my mind was strong. It was going to be hard, but I had never done things the easy way. I'd always done things the Dana way, with passion and drive, and I was going to tackle my recovery the same way. Step by step, just like the Whitney Houston song I woke up to. I was going to win, no matter how much it hurt.

chapter 9

GOING HOME

From about the first month after the burn I didn't have a face. It was hidden from the world by my mask. For 23 and a half hours a day, I wore a pressure mask and garment designed to control scarring. The garment put even pressure over my entire body in order to flatten the scars by reducing blood flow to the skin, starving the scars of resources. It also physically forced them down, depriving them of room to raise too far off the body. Pressure garments are an incredibly important part of burns recovery, the frontline defence against debilitating scarring for most survivors. But wearing a pressure garment is exactly as comfortable as it sounds.

The first time the nurses fit me into it, I couldn't believe how uncomfortable it was. It was so, so painful – like wearing the tightest bra you've ever worn, but around your whole body. And I wore it constantly. Once a day someone would help me out of it so I could wash. I couldn't even do the garment up or put my gloves on myself. I'd be stripped naked, showered as though I were a baby, with someone – a nurse, my sister, my mother – helping me in and out of a special showering chair, and then I'd be straight back into the garment. Any more time than that and my scarring would worsen.

It's hard to convey just how much pain I was in. My nerves had been completely destroyed and, while they'd grown back, they'd done so in, as my doctors put it, a 'less than normal' way. Because my nerves were growing back into a body that had been fundamentally changed – a complex assortment of original skin, grafted flesh and scar tissue – I've ended up with broken and dead nerves that basically cause chaos in the pain receptors of my nervous system. As I healed, I developed a condition called allodynia, a chronic level of hypersensitivity, which meant my pain response to the slightest touch was out of all proportion to the stimulus. On any of the grafted skin the slightest sensation – a feather brushing against me, a slight breeze – would cause ripples of agony all through my system.

No matter how gentle my nurses and family were, there was no way they could avoid hurting me every single day. One time when I was showering, with Svetlana helping me in and out, I turned too quickly and slipped out of my chair, knocking my arm on the glass door of the shower.

It was only a gentle little knock but I may as well have been hit with an axe. I howled with pain and saw that a massive gash had opened up on the grafted skin. Blood started pouring down into the drain. Svet had to hurry to get me out of the shower and stop the bleeding, and I still remember the look in her eyes, just the sheer sorrow and desperation of the situation we'd found ourselves in. Her heart was breaking and may as well have been pouring down the drain along with all the blood. It was so hard to see how much my injuries were hurting the people who loved me. Sometimes I felt even more trapped by those feelings than by the compression suit.

Another thing that was worse than the pain was the itch. Oh God, *that itch*. As much as the flames, that itch haunts me. I have lost more sleep to the itch than to any of my injuries and operations. And I couldn't even scratch myself, because my arms were ruined and locked down by the scars.

I would beg my mum and sister to scratch me, but when they did, huge flakes of skin would come off, and more often than not I would start bleeding, so they didn't like doing it. That didn't stop me, though. I was obsessed. When nobody was looking I would try to find ways to scratch myself. Mum would come into the ward and I would be rubbing up against the corners of furniture like a cat. It was out of control. Later, when I could go out in public, I would run up to strangers in the street, this wild-eyed woman in a compression suit and a mask, and ask,

'Can you scratch my back? Scratch my itch! Go on!' And some of them, God bless them, would do it!

It was enough to make me crazy. The itch is a bitch, enough said. But the mask and the garment were essential for my recovery. Without them, I was as good as doomed, so I learnt to welcome the itch as I had welcomed the pain.

After more than four months in hospital, when Dale, Suzanne and the rest of the team were satisfied with my health, I was transferred into out-patient care. That meant I was allowed to go home. I would still have to come into the hospital every day for treatment and therapy, but I could at least sleep in my own bed – even if it was the bed from my childhood, in my old room at Mum's house, and I would still have to sleep in an upright crucifix position.

I wouldn't be going back to my apartment ever again. While I was still in hospital, my landlord had cancelled the lease and my stuff had been put into storage. But even if my little apartment had still been there waiting for me, I wouldn't be able to live alone any time soon.

I was completely physically handicapped. I couldn't feed myself, change my clothes, go to the toilet, shower or even blow my nose. Mum picked me up from the hospital, drove me back to her house and, with her arm around my waist, helped me limp inside. I couldn't even walk without her.

It was a beautiful day, though, because I was reunited with the love of my life, Killer. Before I came in, I made Mum close the sliding door that separated the back of the house from the front. I wanted to surprise Killer and see if he recognised my voice, because it felt like I'd been in hospital and hadn't seen him for an eternity.

'Killer!' I called softly. 'It's me!'

The poor little thing went berserk, yelping with joy and anticipation, trying to batter down the door to get to me. Mum opened the door and he came barrelling at me, leaping up to try to lick my face. He'd missed me as much as I'd missed him. I couldn't stop crying. Soon my mask was completely soaked by tears, but I didn't care. I was back with my little Killer.

From then on, it was me, Mum and Killer in the house. Mum gave up everything to look after me, even her job at the hospital. Looking after me was a full-time occupation, and then some. I couldn't get out of bed without her help, let alone manage the dozens of tasks I needed to go through every day in order to recover and stay infection-free. She would get me up, take off my garments, put healing creams and gels on my scars, and massage them three times a day. This was a special therapeutic massage that involved pressing your fingertips into the scar until it started to turn white, rubbing the area with firm pressure while applying a special cream designed to provide more flexibility and soften the skin. In hospital, the nurses would perform this massage three times a day, and then Mum had to do the same. At least three times a day, for three years.

It was a huge responsibility, but so much of my life was at stake. The massages and cream were designed to keep the skin from drying out and to help with the elasticity of the scar. It basically kept my skin soft enough that it wouldn't crack while I did my stretches and lifted therapeutic weights. And it slowly helped to release the broken and dead nerves in the scar tissue that – over several years – would help to reduce my hypersensitivity to pain.

After each massage, Mum would dress me again in the pressure garments and heave me up into bed. And she's a tiny woman! She did all of this, all the back-breaking physical effort of helping me heal, without a second thought. Basically, she did everything except breathe for me, bless her.

'You know what?' she said one day, as she was helping me into bed. 'You are more work now than when you were a baby.' It was true. For the longest time, her entire existence revolved around keeping me alive. She never complained, but it must have been incredibly stressful. Even the good times, the times when we should have been celebrating, were tinged with sorrow.

Without my mum I wouldn't have lasted a day. I couldn't do anything for myself, so Mum did everything for me.

But at least I was back with my family. My mum, my sister and my son, who, technically speaking, was my dog. I'd been away from Killer for too long, and I spent every minute I could with him. I was housebound, but I would take him on little walks through the house, shuffling along while he yapped and scampered around my feet. When I sat down, he would leap up into my arms. I would pat

Svet always had my back even
when we were little.

Ready for my close-up on
Koolan Island.

Left to right: my big sisters, Suzie and Svetlana, me, and my twin brother, Denis.

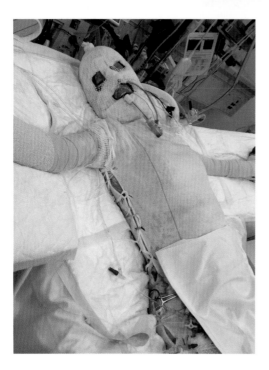

In the burns unit at the Royal Perth Hospital after the attack.

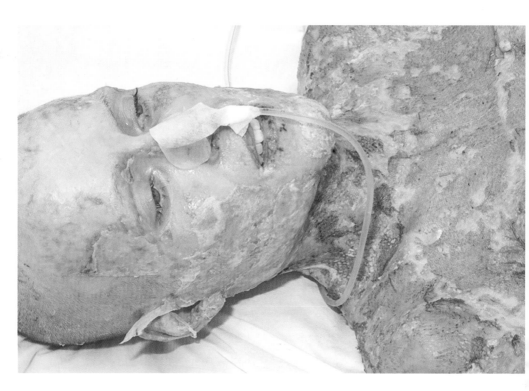

Waking from my coma with burns to two-thirds of my body, I had the fight of my life ahead of me.

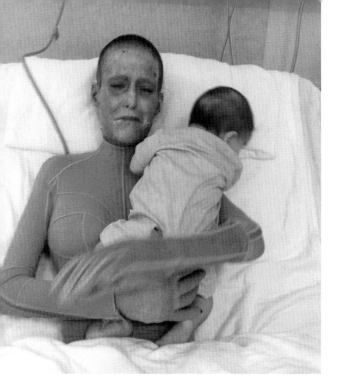

My heart breaking as I try to hold my little nephew. I was too badly burned to touch his skin.

Fighting the scar. Every day meant hours of agonising physiotherapy to regain mobility.

LEFT: I'm a survivor – there's no way I was going to let that burn beat me.

BELOW: Fashion forward in compression garment chic.

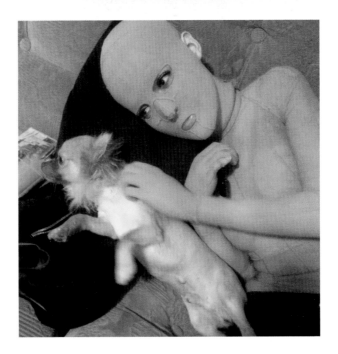

Me and Killer, the love of my life, chilling on the couch.

Mum, me and Svet leaving the courtroom after my assailant was finally brought to justice.

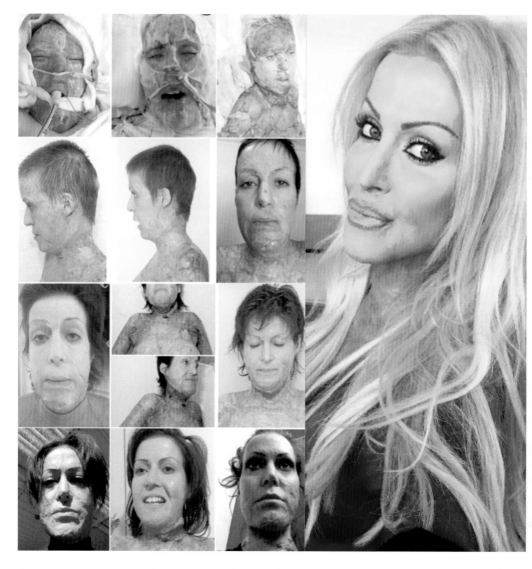

My journey of recovery. I post these before-and-after photos to show other survivors what is possible if you never give up. Hope is the most important gift you can give – and receive.

TOP LEFT: Me and Svet at the Men in Black ball in June 2015, raising awareness for men's mental health.

TOP RIGHT: With my mum, Vera, after I'd just hosted WA's biggest International Women's Day lunch in March 2017.

BOTTOM LEFT: Peace! My recovery is nearly complete, but my story has only just started. Watch this space.

I've learned to love my body more than ever because of everything we've been through together: the battle to become Dana again. Every day is a gift and that's worth fighting for.

him as best I could as I wailed all this gibberish, thanking him for being the best puppy in the world.

If I know one thing for certain, one piece of life advice that's the absolute truth – and I tell this to everyone who's been through trauma, who faces a long, tough recovery: get a pet, if you're able to. Get a little dog, a little pure-hearted puppy like Killer. It makes you happier. It makes life so much easier. It gives you something to live for.

Coming home, I had two big surprises. The first was that Killer was waiting for me to brighten my life. The other was that the media was waiting for me too, but to ruin my life. That was something I hadn't reckoned with during my time in the hospital, and I had no idea until I was confronted with the fact of it. I was suddenly, very much against my will, a news story.

chapter 10

BEHIND THE MASK

Most of the time I'd been in hospital I wasn't allowed to watch TV, and especially not the news. There was a TV in my room, but the staff were instructed to not let me watch it. When I asked why, someone let slip that the hospital had decided it would be best to protect my psychological state, especially while my physical prognosis was so uncertain. All information about the outside world was carefully controlled.

At first I thought it was because there had been some kind of disaster – a tsunami or earthquake or terrorist attack, something so horrible they didn't want me worrying about it while I was concentrating on my recovery. As it turns out, they didn't want me watching the news because I was all over it.

When I was burnt, it was front-page news. It was just

such a sensational story – a young blonde woman attacked at random, the gruesome nature of the violence, the revelation that the attacker was on ice, her dramatic arrest at the airport. It could have happened to anyone and that's what made it so frightening. Young women could picture it happening to them and parents worried about the safety of their daughters on the street. It was a like a horror film, but it was my life.

One thing that really annoyed me, though, was that so many people seemed most concerned about my 'pretty face' and about me losing my looks. What about me as a person, and my functionality, and the impact on my loved ones?

I was shocked to find that while I'd been in hospital fighting for my life, the media had been following my story every step of the way. Now that I was home, now that they finally had a chance to get photos for their tabloids, the media camped outside my home 24/7.

They were following every little aspect of my story. Every time a new fact came to light they pounced on it like a pack of wolves with a piece of meat, and if there was no new information they would just make something up. Otherwise, they just hung out trying to take paparazzi snaps of me when I went to hospital. I would be limping to the car, in full pressure garment and mask, and Mum and Svet would be trying to shield me with a newspaper or blanket.

They even bothered my poor family at the hospital, in the first weeks when I was still in the coma. Obviously they couldn't get into the ICU ward where I was being treated, but they were still lurking around every corner, waiting for their chance. On the second day after the burn, Svet had visited my bedside, seen my ruined body, and had just been told by the doctors that it was by no means certain I would survive. She held it together long enough to have that impossible conversation with the doctors, but then broke down in the hallway in tears.

There is a church across the road from the hospital, St Mary's Cathedral; a big, calm place to pray. Svet decided to head there to get some solace, just a few minutes alone to cry and scream and ask God why this had happened to her sister. She was blind with tears, snuffling and screaming on her way to the church when she realised a pack of photographers had followed her the whole way. They just wouldn't give us a moment of peace. It was so stressful, and so unfair on my family. None of us signed up for this.

The media made it especially hard for poor Mum. Whenever she saw them camped out in our front yard she would run outside and chase them off. They would back off 10 metres or so and then set up again, so the whole process would start over. It was a bit like that game 'What's the time, Mr Wolf?' Mum was trying hard to protect me, and they did not give her a minute of peace.

At times, overwhelmed by what had happened, and the sheer work it took to keep me alive, she would need to cry. But she would never do it in front of me. She'd tell herself,

'I have to be strong in front of Dana.' So she would go for a little drive to find a place to cry, only to have some photographer jump out at her. It went on for a long, long time. I don't know what they were hoping for – I wasn't about to put on a show for them. It's not like I'd be going out clubbing.

Being under siege from the media was not conducive to the healing process. Their obsession with getting a picture of me without my mask on was a constant reminder that my life had changed forever. My mask and I were developing a strong love-hate relationship. While I respected it, and understood it was helping me to recover as best I could, the psychological toll of wearing it was huge. It made me feel faceless, like a nothing – a not-person. When you are badly burnt, you already suffer from a disconnect between the way you look and the way you feel. In my mind, I was Dana Vulin: a young, independent woman. When I looked in the mirror: a melted satay-peanut. It's common in burns survivors – the difference between who you are and what you look like is so alienating. And it's even worse to go for years on end looking in the mirror and just seeing a beige, emotionless nothing staring back at you.

After many months of being trapped at home and in my mask, I was quietly going mad. I'd once taken such joy in expressing myself through the way I looked and dressed, and now every day I was in the same awful body suit – talk about being a fashion repeater.

I remember being on the phone to Jackie, telling her how miserable I was, limping around the house in compression bandages and tracksuit pants.

'Every single day, it's the same outfit. I can't do makeup, I can't do my hair. It's torture,' I vented.

'So what do you want to do about it?'

'Let's go shopping!'

Jackie picked me up in her car and we quickly ditched the paparazzi so we could have a little privacy. We decided to go the Belmont Forum, a shopping centre, to check out some of the boutiques there. We were convinced that with our combined powers we could find something to funk up my compression suit. We parked around the back and snuck in through the rear entrance, just in case any media happened to be lurking out the front.

I was feeling very shy and insecure, as well as physically frail, but for a little while I was able to forget the situation I was in and just have a nice time with Jackie. I felt just like a regular person – out in the world of hustle and bustle and Kmart and Boost Juice.

We went to one boutique, then another, and we were going through the racks when a security guard came up to us.

'I'm going to have to ask you to leave,' he said to me. I just stared at him, shocked – not that he could tell through the mask.

'Why?'

'You need to take that mask off.'

'I can't.'

He ignored me and turned to Jackie, pointing at me. 'She needs to take that mask off or leave,' he told her. 'She's a security risk.'

'Listen!' I said, trying not to cry. 'I can't take it off. It's a medical mask. I need it to recover.'

'I don't believe you.'

'Dude,' I insisted, 'I got burnt.'

'Well then, you shouldn't be out here shopping.'

'Don't worry about that jerk,' Jackie told me as we left the shop. 'I'll buy you lunch.'

She tried her best to cheer me up, but I was badly hurt. We bought sushi for lunch but I couldn't even really eat that. I had to lift my mask halfway up to fit the sushi in my mouth, and even then it was hard for me to chew. All the while I could feel a hundred eyes staring at me, and that horrible security guard glaring at us from across the food court. I'd hoped that a shopping trip would make me feel less alienated, but thanks to that guy I felt even worse.

I spent every day in the mask and garment, and every day wishing I could rip them off and just throw them in the trash. Apart from the agony and the itch, the worst part about it was that I had to wear the same thing for three years. I'm the sort of woman who likes to rock what she wears – I would always look immaculate, always switch it up, always be my best. And here I was stuck in fashion hell for three years.

The garment wasn't even black, which is a timeless classic. It was beige! And ironically, the year I had finally recovered enough to throw the thing away, beige came into fashion. What can I say? I was ahead of my time as usual; just too cool for school.

Although, you know what? When the time came, when I could finally start wearing normal clothes and stop wearing those garments, I didn't throw them all away. I got rid of most of them, but I've kept a couple, almost like a security blanket. And honestly, after all that time, I love those garments as much as I hate them. Or at least, I respect them for what they've given me. Without my pressure garments I would have been completely fused into one little ball. The garment at least gave me the shape of a human being, and a fighting chance for a normal life.

Same with the mask. For years I hated that mask for taking away my personality. I had no eyebrows, no nose, no facial expressions, nothing. All you could see of my face were my eyeballs and my tiny, shrivelled mouth. Until your face is taken away from you, you don't realise how much you depend on it to express your personality. Your features are who you are and, essentially, I had become a blank canvas. The experience of talking to someone and seeing them struggling to understand me through the mask was all too common.

So I wore the mask, and the garment, day in and day out. I did the hard yards. I've not known anyone else to wear the garments that long – but I knew where I wanted to go and what it would take to get there. I could have taken them off earlier, but I wanted to squeeze every little bit of help from them that I could. My burns were extraordinarily bad, so they required an extraordinary response. If wearing the garments for another year meant reducing even one scar, then I would wear them for another year. It's a long road. Longer than you can imagine. Longer than I could have imagined, at the start of it all. Early on after the attack, I was still replying to invitations to parties that were months away. 'Of course I'll be there,' I told my friends. I told myself the same thing. Of course, when it rolled around, I was not at that party – I was in intensive therapy grappling with the fact that I might never be able to hold a pencil again.

Then I'd thought to myself, '*Well, these scars are going to take two years to mature, so I'm going to put aside two years to recover.*' Two years sacrificed to get my life back – at the time it seemed to be a tough but fair deal. That turned out to be naive. In time I would push that goal back again, and again, to five years and counting. I would give up five years of my life, working 24/7/365 to get back to being the Dana I once was.

I couldn't believe that I'd come so far and worked so hard and was still so broken. Every day I battled with my scars and every day we wrestled to a draw. On some days there was a little improvement, an almost immeasurable amount, a tiny fragment of range of movement returned or the slightest reduction in a scar. These felt like small victories but they were indications I could eventually win the war, despite the endless setbacks.

Meanwhile, life was passing me by. While I worked to heal every day, I was missing out on all those events, big and small, that make up a life. In the middle of 2013 a beloved aunt passed away, but I couldn't make it to the funeral because I was having surgery that day. Friends started dating new people, fell in love, got married, had children. Every bit of good news filled me with joy, but it was a joy tinged with sadness, because I couldn't be there in the way that I wanted.

I'm not going to lie, some of those days were really dark. Mum was there for the worst of my recovery and I could see that she was concerned about me. She was worried that I would lose the will to live, that I would make a choice not to go on fighting. Her biggest fear when I was still in the coma was that when I came out of it I would not want to live. And now, caring for me full time, seeing the agony that survival would put me through – then and in the future – she was terrified that I was going take my own life. She never said anything, but I figured it out by the way she would never want to leave me alone, not even for five minutes, the fear in her eyes when she had to pop out and the relief when she came back. To see your mum overcome with relief that you haven't killed yourself while she was out buying milk? It breaks both your hearts. I had to sit her down and say, 'Mum, you can go to the shops for half an hour, it's fine. I'm not going to do anything dumb.'

Was I upset? Yes, of course, who wouldn't be? Would it have been easier to die? Yes, way easier. Did I think about killing myself? No, never. Not for one second.

The tragic fact is that a lot of burn survivors do struggle with depression and end their own lives. It's so sad, but I can understand: the mental agony you go through, the shock, the sadness of knowing your life will never be the one you'd always hoped for. And the physical agony – the endless chronic pain as your shattered body tries to piece itself together. It really is hell on earth, and nobody deserves to live like that.

But I'd resolved, back when I was in the burns ward, to face it head-on. Obviously there were times when I was really angry and sad and wanted to quit, but that's just human nature. I was going to beat this.

I may have struggled, but I've never once been on antidepressants. I'm certainly not saying that there is anything wrong with antidepressants, and many people do benefit from them, but I know my body and mind, and am convinced that this particular treatment option is not for me. While I was in the burns unit, a fellow inpatient used antidepressants. She used to take them at 9 a.m. on the dot every morning. If she overslept, she would wake up crying her eyes out. When I asked her what was wrong she told me between sobs, 'I can just think so clearly, and realise everything that's happened, and really see it for what it is.' The shock for her was the same every time she missed her medication, and I decided that if I was going to beat my burn I needed to be able to see the situation clearly. If I knew the devil I was dealing with then I could kick it in the face.

I couldn't stop fighting. Even in my lowest moments, my heart wouldn't let me give up hope. I felt I owed it to my family, and the surgeons and physios who had worked so hard to not only save my life but to give me back a life worth living. And I especially had to fight for my mum and sister. The sacrifices they were making, the amount of life they were giving up for me to get mine back – I could never let them down by quitting. Also, I wasn't about to do Natalie's work for her. She'd tried to kill me and failed; I wasn't going to finish the job for her. There is a great saying I read once: 'They tried to bury you but they didn't know you were a seed.' I didn't just want to grow, I wanted to flourish!

On the bad days, I just had to swallow my tears and get on with working on my recovery. My old life was gone and I would have to build a new one. And to do that, I was going to need something that was becoming the most precious thing in my life: hope.

chapter 11

BURNS RETREAT

About five and half months after I was burnt I attended my first burns retreat – a weekend away for burns survivors. It was run by the Peter Hughes Burn Foundation, a not-for-profit that supports victims of burns trauma and their families. As an organisation, they're all about education and empowerment. They help survivors learn how to identify their strengths and weaknesses, and support each of us in developing a 'toolbox' of coping strategies and techniques relevant to our individual needs.

The organisation was originally founded by Peter Hughes, a man who survived the Bali Bombings and unwittingly became the face of that attack. A clip of him all messed up from the injury and waiting for treatment was televised around Australia. In it, a reporter asked him how he was feeling, to which he, staunch as anything despite having just been blown up, told the cameras, 'I'm good.' During his recovery, he reinvented himself as a motivational speaker, and he'd become a beacon of hope for people in my situation.

These camps had been set up as a way for the burns community to support each other and share our experiences, and to help us achieve a better quality of life. My medical team, and especially Dale – who by now I'd learnt to trust with my life – assured me it would be a good experience, that it was exactly what I needed to move forward.

'Go meet some other survivors,' Dale urged me. 'Nobody else on earth knows what you're going through like these people do.'

Svetlana drove me up to the camp. We were supposed to stay there for a few nights, getting to know other survivors, basically making friends and forming networks. Although every burn recovery is unique – with its own personalised problems, goals and obstacles to be overcome – it helps to be able to call someone who will understand at least something of what you're going through. Burns are unlike any other injury. They just keep going and going, throwing up more secondary and tertiary health complications.

Even Svet, who sacrificed everything and suffered every wound with me on the whole horrible journey, couldn't *really* understand what it's like. She was my hands, legs, mouth, for years on end – she knows my body and injuries almost as well as I do – but it's still nice to have a friend to call up and bitch about how itchy a compression garment can get. That kind of thing, that sense that someone else out there knows what you're going through, is really important for your psychological health.

My first meeting at the burns retreat was anything but empowering, though. I feel so bad saying this, but when I met my first group of long-term burns survivors, I freaked out. Five months in, I was still getting used to my mask and compression garment, and I was still struggling with my new body. At that point, deep down, I still hadn't really come to grips with how badly hurt I was. I'd spoken to my doctors and I knew that my scars would only mature and worsen, but in my heart I'd never *believed* it. Somewhere deep down I guess I still thought that I was going to be that one survivor who made a miraculous recovery. That hope evaporated very quickly at the first group seminar.

As I was sitting in the big circle, looking around at all the burns survivors as they shared their stories and talked about various ways they'd learnt to survive, I started to panic. In that moment, I couldn't hear the stories of survival or understand the bravery of those people. Instead, I saw people with severe deformities – people who'd lost fingers, limbs, others with missing noses or ears, those who'd been blinded or lost their whole face to scarring. For the first time, I saw what my future probably looked like, and all I could feel was horror. I feel terrible, remembering that. Each and every one of those people is amazing, an absolute hero, but in that moment it was all too much and I had to leave the room. Once I was safely outside I collapsed, leaning against the wall and sobbing my eyes out.

It all seemed so unfair. Nobody in that room had chosen to be there. Nobody deserved to be burnt. They were all normal people, just like me, with the same dreams and hopes and fears as anybody. Whatever lives they'd been planning had been snatched away by pain and scarring. That thought made the tears uncontrollable and I started crying even harder. My arms were still pinned down by scars at that point, so I couldn't even wipe away my tears. I just had to let them fall.

After a while I became aware that someone was watching me, a woman who'd followed me out from the seminar and was standing by while I got all my tears out. She watched me quietly, and then she moved forward to comfort me. As she got closer, I saw that she had no fingers on her hands – they had mostly been burnt off.

'What's the matter?' she asked. 'Why are you crying?'

'It's nothing,' I replied. I didn't want to be rude and tell her that I was horrified by the people in there and that I was sad because this was my future. 'It's really nothing.'

'It's pretty scary, huh?' she said, waving her hands in front of me.

I started laughing, and then talking, and I was pleased to find this woman shared the exact same sense of humour as me.

That was how I first met Caroline Mayer. Talk about inspirational. A genuine, darling, super-cool person.

Caroline was everything you could ever want in another person: caring, kind, funny and, best of all for me, vulgar. She was blessed with a really brilliant and filthy personality, same as me – she was instantly a soul sister to me.

That first day of the camp, she helped me pull myself together and immediately took me under her wing. I think she recognised that I was freaked out and needed help with everything. She was that for me from day one, without ever asking for anything in return. When Svet had to leave suddenly to look after her baby, Caroline stepped up.

'Don't worry,' she told Svet. 'It's all good. I'll take care of her.'

That night Caroline helped me with my dressings – taking off my garment and helping me into the shower and the toilet, then treating me with all the creams and bandages that were holding my shattered body together. After that, she helped me get my garment back on and tucked me into bed. Believe me when I tell you this was a superhuman effort. Because of the intense pressure of the garment, it's very difficult to climb in and out of. On a good day, it took two nurses to get it on – each nurse grabbing a zip on either side and pulling them up. And Caroline did it all for me by herself. As she did, she was chatting away like we'd been friends for years. She showed me there were no limitations.

Later on she told me the story of how she'd been burnt. She was at home one night in February 2000 and a house fire broke out. She was a young mum, just thirty-three, and her rental property had no working smoke alarm. By the time she woke up, the house was engulfed in flames. She escaped, but then realised that she'd been separated from her little boy – he was still inside the house. Despite the flames she charged back in, only to find the metal security gates into the building had locked behind her after she'd escaped, trapping her son inside the burning house. Through sheer bravery and strength, she managed to force the gate open and rescue her son. She carried him out, miraculously, without a scratch on him. But she was badly hurt, sustaining burns to over 80 per cent of her body, and her hands had pretty much been lost in the struggle to get back into the house.

They'd given her a 50/50 chance of survival, and Caroline spent eight weeks in the Royal Brisbane and Women's Hospital ICU in a coma, followed by nine months of painful recovery in the burns unit. All that time she was separated from her son, and it was the thought of him that kept her fighting to stay alive. When she finally saw him again, she was so physically changed by the burn he no longer recognised her.

Despite the terrible outlook and the loneliness, isolation and grief, she was determined to get her life back. She endured more than a hundred operations and the agony of rehabilitation in order to get back her ability to do the things she'd always been able to do. And here she was, looking after me with as much care and skill as any medical professional. It was very humbling to meet a woman like that. She's a real gift to the world, and to me.

So while that first burns camp was a shock, I did get things out of it I never thought I would. I met Caroline, obviously, and a bunch of other really wonderful people. But more than any of that, what I took away from the camp was motivation.

After meeting Caroline and hearing her story, I realised that if I didn't do something extreme – really go at my recovery like a crazy person and work my titties off – then I would become defined by my burns. My injuries were extreme, but I have always been an extreme person, so that was fine. If my burns were extreme, if my scars were above average, then I would have to force myself to have an above-average recovery. After the camp, on my way home with Svet, I turned to her in the car and told her what I needed to do. 'I'm going to beat this,' I assured her.

So I had motivation, but I was now desperate for inspiration. The sort of transformation that I wanted to achieve, from my current state to where I wanted to be, seemed almost impossible. But maybe there was someone out there who'd come close. Together, Svet and I searched high and low for this kind of inspiration, and finally we discovered Katie Piper.

Katie is a TV presenter and former model from England. She'd been on track for a full-time career in the media, but then she had sulphuric acid thrown in her face by an attacker. The whole thing had been arranged by a jealous ex-boyfriend. Afterwards, she'd fought like hell to get her face back, undergoing a world-first operation to have all the skin on her face removed and replaced with a graft, and another brand-new operation to restore her vision. And she went on to have the media career she'd always worked towards, which was inspirational in itself. But the thing that really made me pay attention was how hard she'd worked to get her face back. She was beautiful before the attack, and now she was beautiful again. And through it all she'd been stunning on the inside.

There were actually a lot of parallels in our circumstances. We were both attacked because of jealousy. We were both blonde and 25. We had very similar personality types and backgrounds. We even had the same kind of dog! The main difference was, while she'd already been in recovery for a while now, I was just getting started. She'd come so far, undergone such a dramatic change for the better. I decided that I wanted that, and even more if possible.

I would do whatever it took. Like Katie Piper, I would go to any length, seek any treatment, no matter how far-out, in order to get closer to the best Dana I could be. And like Caroline, I would do it for my family. Caroline refused to give up on life, because she had a little boy who needed her. My family had invested so much care, time, love and faith in my recovery – I was determined to get my life back so I could share it with them.

I guess it was meeting Caroline, seeing someone who had endured so much and come through it, not just undiminished but actually stronger, that gave me a real kick up the arse. She inspired me to do whatever the fuck I needed to do. I would learn from her, and from Katie Piper, and from everyone else out there who's been through hell and come out the other side. And when I was done, when my recovery was complete and I had my fully functioning body back, I would return to the burns retreats as a survivor, ready to pass on what I knew to a new generation of survivors, just like Caroline had been a symbol of hope for me.

I don't think I ever told her that, but I've always had a great love and respect for her. She had given me hope, which is the greatest possible gift. I know that she saved my life, as surely as my doctors and my family did. And I knew that one day I could be that person for others.

chapter 12

LITTLE VICTORIES

If there's one good thing that comes out of going through terrible suffering, it's that it really gives you perspective on what's important in life. It makes you understand how many people out there in the world are going through terrible times without anyone to help them.

In early 2013 I watched on the news as bushfires swept through New South Wales, causing close to $94 million worth of damage and taking innocent lives. I was moved by the plight of all the people on the other side of the country whose lives, like mine, had been derailed by fire. My heart went out to them and I began to think about ways I might be able to help. I know, from personal experience, how powerful it is when you're going through hard times and people show you compassion. It gives you hope, and that in turn gives you strength. There had to be something

I could do, even though I was physically broken and financially broke.

It occurred to me that I was sitting on a small fortune in clothes and one-off fashion items I'd collected before the burn. Over the years, I'd accumulated some very rare and lovely items in my wardrobe, and now, while they would be of no more use to me, they could help raise funds for the people whose lives had been turned upside-down by bushfire. I decided to donate my clothes to the St Vincent de Paul Society to help with the relief effort.

I went to pull them out of storage and spent some time sorting through them; my favourite gowns for special occasions, the tops and skirts I once went clubbing in. Some of them were almost famous now – every time the media needed a photo of me to run with a story, they would find one online that had been taken out at a club, smiling in some cute outfit.

I couldn't see a future where I would ever be able to wear them again, but maybe I could give them to someone else to make their own future brighter. Then I started calling around to find other clothes my friends and family could spare. And, thinking of the children I'd seen crying on the news, I tracked down toys from my childhood and packed them away for donation too. As I boxed them up, I thought back to the little girl who'd once played on the beaches of Koolan Island with her brother and sisters.

Among all that I found an old pair of Mum's sunglasses that brought a smile to my face. I remembered my mum and dad trying to nap in the sun while I demanded Mum take a photo of me. I smiled, thinking back to that little girl who was always the centre of attention. If I'd known what it was like to be harassed by the media, I would have been more careful in what I'd wished for. When I was younger, Svet had always told me I'd be a star one day. She didn't know how, but she just knew she was going to see my name up in lights. Now it seemed like the whole world was watching me, but for all the wrong reasons.

Those sunglasses went away with the clothes that I would never wear again. So did the toys. I would keep the memories, but the items belonged to another Dana. The future belonged to a different Dana altogether.

I could let the tragedy cut me down or I could wield it like a sword, fighting every day. The goal was to become an even stronger woman than I was before the burn. One day I would be the version of Dana that I was in the dream that has haunted me since the coma right after the attack: walking into a club wearing that pink dress, even prouder and more powerful than I had been in my old life. I had a goal, but it was going to take everything I had to achieve it, maybe even more than I had.

By this point, I knew enough about recovery to know that the big victories, the things you celebrate, are not the most important moments. It's about every little moment, every achievement, every millimetre of movement claimed back from the scars, every battle to learn how to do the smallest things again; they all add up. So I put together very clearly defined goals that I wanted to achieve – to be able to do the small, normal things – because they would turn out to be the sweetest victories. To be able hold my phone to my face; to stop having to wear gloves to touch my phone and actually be able to answer a call. I would become stronger than I had ever been, even if I had to crawl there. But first I had to learn how to crawl.

A year and a half after the burn, I achieved one of my big personal goals. Mum had helped me into the shower and then left me alone under the water while she went off to take care of something. I sat under the water, helpless, and looked at my hands curled up uselessly in front of me. It was a little under thirteen months after the best burns team on the planet had told me I would probably never regain much of my movement, that I might never even be able to hold a pencil again. I had battled day and night ever since to prove them wrong. The massages, the physiotherapy, the hard-core surgeries, the endless agonising exercises – all of that. But I was still so helpless. I decided to push it, then and there, and started trying to force my hand up to my face. I struggled, my feeble muscles against the scar, sheer force of will against the pain. '*I will touch my face*,' I thought. '*I will do it now.*' I started crying out in pain as the skin started to split and tear where skin grafts and scar tissue met, but I kept going. That day, like every day, it was now or never.

Mum heard me screaming from the other side of the house. 'Mum! Mum!' She started running to find me, thinking maybe I'd fallen over and broken a limb, but she found me in the shower, naked, red and raw, with one triumphant finger held to the side of my face.

'Look, Mum!' I was sitting there, blood running down my arms and pooling at the bottom of the shower, tears streaming down my face. 'Look, Mum!' I yelled again, as excited and proud as that little girl on the beach twenty-five years before. 'I can touch my face! I did it!'

Mum burst into tears and helped me out of the shower. For a while I stayed there, crying with joy (and from pain, sure, heaps of it, but also joy). It might not seem like a big deal, but just imagine it. For nearly a year and a half, I'd been completely helpless – if my face was itchy, or I needed to adjust my mask, I couldn't do it. My friend Stella used to mess with me when we were hanging out by reaching out and pulling little tufts of hair out through the ear-hole of my mask. I looked a bit like a real-life Homer Simpson. Every time I saw her, if I let my guard down for a second, *bam*, she'd pounce and mess with my hair, and I would have to ask someone else to fix it. Now, with just this little bit of movement back, I knew that soon I would be able to fix my own damned hair, and a million other things. After the horrible weekend in the ward, when I'd lost nearly all my movement, they told me I might never touch my face again. And now, I could. I could do anything.

Mum was full of joy as well, but a little later on I heard her crying in her room. I realised that while she was as thrilled as I was that I'd fought my way back to having that little bit of movement, it broke her heart that her daughter had to go through this horrible trial. My own heart filled up with the most indescribable sadness as I witnessed how much pain my struggle was causing her. She's a strong woman, amazing and generous, but what had happened to me was wearing her down.

She'd not had a moment's rest since I had been attacked. She had not slept a full night since I'd come home, because my body would start to stiffen up and contract if I stayed in the same position for more than a few hours. So every few hours she would have to wake up, come to my room, wake me up and help me move my body through a series of exercises. Nearly every day she would have to drive me to the hospital, often only to hear more bad news. Can you imagine how painful it must have been for her? To have her little girl back in the house, so badly hurt, and to have to work with her through a new world of agony every day.

Luckily, Svetlana stepped up. She'd been helping with my recovery from day dot, but now she was spending more and more time over at Mum's to give her a break. She'd drive over with her little baby and then spend hours helping with showers, dressing, exercise, massages. She was spending so much time looking after me that, after a while, I started staying at her place across town, even spending nights there now and again. It was the only way Mum could get some much-needed rest, even though she always insisted that she didn't need it, or want to be apart from me.

When I stayed the night at Svet's place I would sleep in her bed with her. A couple of decades earlier, I used to climb into bed with her after I'd had a nightmare, or just when I wanted to hang out with my big sister. And now here we were, sharing a bed again after all these years. Sharing a bed was the only practical solution, though. Every couple of hours I would have to wake up and get turned over, wriggle my fingers, move every muscle I could in an effort to keep my mobility, and it was so much easier if Svet could just wake up and get straight to work

To make room, Svet's husband Filip would give up his bed and go and sleep in the spare top bunk in his five-year-old son's room. Filip is just the kindest, most understanding man you could imagine, so when Svet floated the idea of me coming to stay with them, he said, 'Of course. Whatever we can do.' That's a real man, right there. A total legend.

Please take a minute to try to understand the immense pressure all of this put on Svet. She had a baby who'd been born just weeks before I was attacked, as well as another little boy already, and now she was sharing a bed with her sister who required critical care – and her poor husband had been banished to a bunk bed. All of us were crammed into this tiny little house, out of which Svet and Filip were also trying to run their business, a commercial fit-out installation company that employs twenty people. It made for the most intense household you could imagine. I would wake up and Svet would be nursing the baby while turning me over and moving my limbs to stop me seizing up until our house-visit nurse arrived, meanwhile there were kids running around under our feet and all sorts of family and friends just popping over to say hi.

At one point our grandma, who is a really proper old-school European lady, came over. Svet was burning dinner, my nephew Nanni (the family used to croon the nonsense words *nanni noony* at him as a baby, and slowly that became his nickname) was running around naked, and I was halfway through having my dressings changed. So I'm sitting there at the dining room table half naked with this Hannibal Lecter-looking mask on, like, 'Hi, Grandma!' And she was like, 'What the hell is this?'

It was madness, but honestly, that kind of good, healthy madness is exactly what I needed. My little nephews, especially, brightened every day. No matter how blue I was, they could cheer me up. It did me no end of good to be around those sweet little boys. They didn't look at me with horror or pity, they just saw me as Aunty Dana. They were happy to jump up on my lap and play with me, no matter how messed up I looked. Those were moments of true happiness, having Nanni sit with me while I read him a story. He would have to turn the pages for me, because my hands didn't work well enough, and soon that became another big goal in my life – to turn the pages on the book as I read to the boys.

I kept that goal in mind every time I had to do physio, or have another painful injection, or have my skin and scars cut to provide flexibly. I imaged my little nephew's face as I turned the page to read him the next part of the story.

And then, one day, it happened. I moved my hand, all on my own, pinched the page, and flipped it.

Again, it might seem small, but it was the end of a long, torturous journey and a major victory for me. My nephew had no idea of what a big deal it was, he was just enjoying his story, but that's the point. Once they've been taken away from you, getting the smallest, simplest things back is the sweetest feeling.

For example: you should have seen the party Svet and I had the day I learnt how to wipe my own arse. Goddamn, that was a beautiful day. Svet and I danced (well, rocked from side to side, which is as close as I could get) around the room in pure joy, high-fiving each other. After I'd washed my hands, of course.

I really believe you don't know true happiness until you've known true despair. On days like that, I knew I could beat anything. Not long ago the doctors had thought I could be functionally immobile for life, and now I was one step closer to full independence.

And Svet? Svet would never have to wipe her sister's butt ever again.

Those were the good times, but you'd best believe that every single one of those victories came at a huge cost. Countless hours of physio, even more of massage, indescribable amounts of pain and, most daunting of all, going under the knife.

But there was something on the horizon that would probably be the biggest challenge of all – one that kept me up at night even more than the blinding pain and the maddening itch. My assailant's case was going before the court and my chance to tell my story was, at long last, just around the corner.

chapter 13

COURT

The trial started in July 2013. Natalie Dimitrovska was charged with grievous bodily harm with intent. I don't think I've ever been more nervous in my life. I was going to testify and I knew that it was not going to be easy.

I was sick – literally sick – with worry. The thought of being in the same room as my assailant, of having to look her in the eye, filled me with anxiety and anticipation. In the days leading up to the trial, my stomach was in knots and my heart was beating so much and so fast, it actually ached. The toll it took on my body was huge. As the date got closer the stress started to mess with my concentration and my rehabilitation started to suffer. I grew weaker, and exhausted. The worry about what would happen in court was like a physical weight on my back, pushing me down as I dragged myself through my exercises every day.

My health suffered, and I was plagued with skin infections and abscesses. In the week of the trial, I had a golf-ball sized abscess on my left shoulder that hurt so much I had to walk hunched over.

My fear was heightened by some lawyer friends of mine who warned me that when they take the stand the victims of crime are often treated as though they are the guilty ones. Because of the assumption of innocence – the idea that everyone accused of a crime is considered innocent until proven otherwise – it would be up to me and the prosecution to show that Natalie had tried to murder me. And, in order to prove otherwise, her lawyers would do everything they could to discredit and humiliate me.

To take my mind off it, my family took me to see *Disney On Ice*. I'd barely been out in public since my embarrassing mistreatment by the security guard at the shopping centre and this was supposed to be a real treat. Every woman has a guilty pleasure – mine is Disney movies. They've always filled me with a simple joy that hasn't changed or diminished since I was a little girl.

I was looking forward to that show so much. We had great seats. But because of the stress and anticipation of the court case, I couldn't enjoy it. I was constantly running over what would happen, what I might be asked – I was completely exhausted by the time we sat down. I tried to focus on the skaters, the story, but the next thing I knew, Mum was nudging me awake. I'd fallen asleep in my seat. It was only six o'clock. I'm a night owl, and I hardly ever go to sleep before midnight, but with the anticipation of the trial, I was so beat that I fell asleep right there in front of Aladdin and Jasmine, all swaddled in my pressure garments, breathing heavily like Darth Vader.

The trial had already been delayed because the defence wanted me to turn up and speak without my mask on. My medical team had to convince them that I couldn't. My lawyers advised me that, basically, the defence thought I was exaggerating my injuries. That made me furious. If they had known what I looked like under the mask, the defence would have stopped fighting so hard for me to appear without it. It would have done them no favours for the jury to see the damage that had been inflicted on me. You could see Natalie's guilt written all over my face. In the end, though, my doctors stood firm – I couldn't be without my mask, it would have been too physically damaging.

Secretly, I was relieved. I didn't want the media seeing my face, or for the world to know how badly I'd been hurt. Not until I was ready. I'd been careful to hide from the relentless paparazzi who had been camped outside my family home. There was no way I was revealing my face to the world on their terms. Recovery is hard, and it's supposed to be a private journey, but my privacy had been taken away by the media. When I turned up in court on the first day they were there, a whole pack of them, reporters jostling me with microphones, TV cameras all up in my face.

I wore a big black hooded jacket that covered most of my mask and body and just pushed through, helped by my mum and Svet who protected me as best they could from the media, like they were my bodyguards. I had so many conflicting feelings about the trial. I was nervous and I was scared – but most of all I was relieved that this part of my journey would be over soon. I would finally have a chance to tell my truth.

I had some seriously mixed emotions going into the trial. My mind was plagued by doubt, excitement, fear: a hundred different feelings. But in the moment, as I pushed past the media and limped into the courtroom, they all condensed into one: determination. I was going to tell the world what my assailant had done. A court of law would hear what had happened and justice would be served. Most importantly, Natalie would never hurt anyone again. My friend Stella had said to me, 'This is your one chance to get her with your words and the truth.'

Before I went in my friends decorated me for good luck, like a bride walking down the aisle – or like a warrior going into battle. I had friends' badges and clips and good luck charms stuck all over me. One put her bridal pin through my mask and some of my girlfriends put hairclips and brooches on the back of my neck brace. I would go onto the stand filled with all their good luck and positive energy. It was quite cute, actually. Me sitting there, telling the horror story of my attack, everyone in court shocked and sombre, the court artist sketching me in my mask – and there's all this crazy good-luck shit pinned to my head.

The trial was to open with my testimony so, finally, I told my story to the world.

I spoke about the threatening phone calls, my confusion over Natalie's anger, the fact that I didn't know her husband, Edin, and could not understand why she'd fixated on me. I went into detail about the calls, from her and from Daniel Stone, about how they told me I was going to be beaten and raped. That she'd threatened to 'ruin my pretty little face'. I spoke about the weeks of harassment and threats leading up to the attack, and how I'd woken up in the early hours of 16 February to find Natalie standing over me. I described how she had threatened and intimidated me, smoked ice in my house, and then backed me into a corner before finally dousing me with a full bottle of methylated spirits and turning me into a human fireball.

At the request of the court, I demonstrated the motion with which Natalie had sprayed the spirits at me, using a rapid back-and-forth action. I described the agony of being burnt alive, and the mocking laughter that echoed through the room as she and Stone escaped through the balcony door. The court heard about the two weeks that I spent in a coma, the horror of waking up to discover what had happened to me, and the chronic pain of my injuries and the battle to recover from them. How my life was now a daily struggle, with my mobility stolen away; how my chin had fused into my chest; that even eighteen months later I could not shower or dress myself. As I spoke, the courtroom went deathly quiet, everyone awed into silence, except for muted sobbing from somewhere behind me. With an effort, I twisted around to see that it was my mum, who was crying as quietly as she could. Often during the trial, when the room fell silent, the only sound was Mum's crying.

The whole time Natalie sat on the bench for the accused and stared daggers at me. Every time I looked over she met my eyes and gave me the evils. I couldn't believe it. Here she was in court, trying to prove to the world that she wasn't a violent person, and she spent the whole time staring at me with hate in her eyes. Honestly, one week of your life where it will pay for you to not look cruel and heartless and you can't even make it through a trial without giving me your crazy-eyes. And when they showed pictures of me immediately after my burn, before the scars had settled in and all my dead flesh had been removed, she twisted in her seat and shielded her eyes. She couldn't even look at the pictures, and really, they weren't that bad at all. They only showed me swollen and scorched immediately after the burn – they didn't show the full extent of my injuries, the nightmare of scars and surgery that I was living through. When I described how she'd laughed at me, she cried, or rather, made a weird noise and twisted her face, like someone trying to bring themselves to tears.

It was all an act. Natalie was sobbing uncontrollably while I spoke, but when we broke for a recess and the jury left the room, the second the door closed behind them, all the sadness left her face, to be replaced by cold anger. It was chilling. It was like watching someone turning their humanity on and off with a switch.

When my lawyer asked me what it had felt like to burn alive, I told the simplest truth I could: 'To describe it best, being burnt alive is probably one of the most excruciating pains you could ever feel, but the aftermath is a million times worse. The flesh of your skin being exposed in the dressings is unimaginable. Hell on earth. I would rather have been dead.'

When I was done giving my testimony, it was time for me to be cross-examined by Natalie's lawyer. The defence lawyer was Hylton Quail – a big guy, heavy-set, with neatly cropped dark hair and a dark suit. He stood up and addressed the jury, telling the men and women that he did not imagine the trial would be pleasant for them, that they would be faced with confronting evidence.

'It's only natural for you to feel a great deal of sympathy for this woman, and antipathy for Natalie,' he told them.

'*No shit*,' I thought, but held my tongue. Then Mr Quail turned to me and started trying to destroy me. He tried to suggest that visitors regularly let themselves into my secure apartment by jumping the fence that backed onto my balcony, which required a climb to reach, like this was the most normal thing in the world. The implication was that Natalie was a friend, someone I'd invited into my home.

'I suggest she didn't threaten you at all,' he said. 'I suggest you are wrong.'

Then he started to ask me about the pepper spray and the taser that the police had found in my apartment. He put it to me that I'd been threatening Natalie with the pepper spray and, scared for her life, she had acted in self-defence. I couldn't believe it. This was how they were going to play it? As if Natalie was the victim? That the prospect of being hit with pepper spray was so terrifying that she'd doused me in flames? My blood boiled, but I stayed calm – no way was I going to lose my temper. I would be calm and graceful in the face of all this disrespect.

I patiently explained that I'd carried the pepper spray with me because I was a girl who often walked home alone late at night. I kept it in a special zip on the side of my bag, always in the same place, because it was a pocket I would know exactly how to locate and could get to quickly if I felt suddenly unsafe. On the night I had been attacked, the spray was safely tucked away in that pocket, all zipped up. The prosecutor asked me if I had attacked Natalie with the pepper spray then put it back in my bag to hide the evidence.

I could not believe this question was coming from a professional lawyer.

'You're asking me if, while I was burning alive, did I have the presence of mind to take a bottle of pepper spray, which has never been used, and put it back in my bag, zip up the pocket, close the bag, then place it carefully back on the floor before tending to my burning flesh?'

He agreed that was what he was asking and even the judge shot him a look like, '*Really, man?*'

'No, sir,' I answered calmly and politely. 'I did not put the pepper spray back in my bag, then think to zip it up before trying to put out my burning body and face.' *My god*, I thought.

Quail kept coming at me, though. Another time, I guess because he was worried that Natalie running away through the back door made her look guilty, he put it to me that it was easier for Natalie to leave through the back door than the front door.

'Again, sir, let me just clarify this,' I asked him. 'You're asking if it was easier for them to run through my apartment, go through the two back doors, jump off the balcony, onto the concrete ramp, and run all the way around to the car park, than it was to walk through the front door?'

'Yes.'

'No, sir, it would've been easier to walk through the front door that was a metre away.' That shut him right up.

The longer I was on the stand, the more my self-worth and confidence kicked in. I knew the truth and I wasn't going to let anyone else break me or change the record. My character is my best asset and my best weapon was the truth. All I had to do was tell it.

I hope Quail was embarrassed. Later on, a lawyer friend of mine said I was ten out of ten on the stand, a textbook-perfect witness. That was awesome to hear, but at the time I was just happy to have told my side of the story. After I'd finished testifying I went home, exhausted but exhilarated.

For the next few days, the prosecution brought the full case to bear on the defendant. The police gave the court a rundown of how, acting on leads gathered after Svetlana's press conference, they'd tried to contact Natalie and Edin, and then, failing that, had tapped their phones. They presented phone intercepts of Natalie discussing dyeing her hair when police told the media they were looking for a blonde. The police witness described how he had learnt that Natalie booked tickets to fly out of the country on a plane that would leave just hours after she'd purchased them. According to the police, she bought the tickets the minute she heard a key witness had been arrested. The officer described her dramatic last-minute arrest at Perth airport and detailed how she had initially denied all allegations: attacking me, threatening me, even knowing who I was. And how she'd changed her story after they told her they had evidence she'd been at my home on the night of the attack.

I was shocked. It sounded like the plot of a Hollywood movie, but somehow this was my life. I was living out the plot of this wild melodrama. It was just crazy – and a lot of this information was news to me. Prior to the trial I hadn't been allowed access to the evidence against Natalie. The thinking was that any solid evidence they had against her might tempt me into changing my version of the story, in an attempt to make sure she was found guilty. They'd kept a lot of information from the media as well; slamming her in the press could have made her look guilty and could have prejudiced the jury. They needn't have worried. She had done everything possible to make herself look guilty.

For all eight days of the trial, damning evidence rained down on Natalie. Forensic experts, DNA, phone records of each threatening call and text, the phone intercepts from the police, a geolocation specialist who placed her exactly where she said she wasn't. The court was shown CCTV footage from around my apartment that proved she'd been stalking me for days. There were statements from eyewitnesses that placed her at the scene. And her own fingerprints placed her at the scene. She'd left the methylated spirits bottle with her prints all over it behind when she fled. She may as well have shot me and left the gun behind as evidence!

They played tape of her police interview from after she'd been arrested. Her performance on the video is a masterclass in stone-cold sociopathy: she's just lying through her teeth. She flat-out denied that she'd been to my apartment on 16 February, the night of the attack. Then the cops showed some pictures taken of me in the hospital, all messed up with a breathing tube down my throat, and she barely flinched.

'How do you feel when you see Dana in that state?' an officer asks in the video.

'It hurts . . . She's someone's daughter,' she replied, 'She's a human being.'

Oh, that hurts? I thought. *Try being burnt alive!*

When they asked her if she deliberately dyed her hair after hearing police were looking for a blonde woman, she got defensive.

'You're saying, "You're guilty so you went and changed your hair colour"?' Natalie asked.

'That's a possibility.'

'No comment.'

They even had a crown witness who was with Natalie and Daniel Stone the night of the assault.

Jessica Mazza was a 25-year-old girl from Perth. She told the court that on the night before the attack, she'd been smoking ice with Natalie's brother. After they'd been getting high for a while, Natalie gave her a lift home. On the way back to Mazza's place they both real-ised they were friends with Daniel Stone, so they phoned him, picked him up, and then drove around for another few hours smoking even more ice. Early in the morning of 16 February, Mazza said, the three of them went to my apartment complex, then walked down the path next to my home to see if any lights were on. When they realised I had company – a big, strong dude who could take care of himself – they drove away. An hour later they came back. In all, they would visit my place three times before finally deciding to break in, smoking ice the whole time. Finding this out at the trial was shocking. It was a disgusting feeling to find out that these creepy strangers had been watching me all night.

Natalie and Daniel Stone went towards the apartment block while Mazza stayed in the car. She waited. After a while Stone called her to ask a question, and a few minutes after that they came running out of the apartment block laughing – then sped away in the car. When Jessica Mazza asked the two of them where they'd been, Natalie stopped laughing and told her that there'd been an accident, that someone had been burnt, and 'do not say anything about this to anyone' or she'd kill her.

I've got to say, I felt a little bit sorry for Jessica Mazza when she was testifying. She'd been part of it all, but now she was seeing me for the first time, what they had done to me, and she was completely distraught. The reality was driven home for her, and it broke her heart. She was a mess. After she testified, someone close to her came up to my friends and family and quietly told them that Mazza would do her best to see that justice was done.

A chemical specialist was called to the stand and asked if Natalie's claim that she'd thrown the bottle of methylated spirits at me in self-defence, by reflex, could be plausible. He refuted the suggestion firmly, saying that the pattern of the burns to me and the apartment indicated that the flammable liquid was directed right at me. Even the way her fingerprints lay on the bottle indicated she'd held the bottle exactly the way I'd said. All the evidence supported my version of events; it all matched up exactly. Honestly, I was surprised how accurately I'd remembered it all. In the year and a half that I'd spent trapped in my ruined body, I'd had plenty of time to go over the events in my head, and after a while a person can start to question their own memory – that it couldn't possibly have been as crazy and cruel as it seemed. But here was all the evidence that it was.

If I was Natalie I would have quit then, pled guilty halfway through, and thrown myself to the judge's mercy. There was not one single witness, not one single shred of evidence, not one piece of paper, not one single document that backed up her story – or even cast her in a good light. Instead, as the evidence mounted, she just sat in the courtroom and glared at me. If looks could kill, she would have put me in the hospital. Again. She showed no remorse.

Finally, the prosecution's case was at an end, and it was time for Natalie to give her version of events. Her lawyer assured us that she denied the charge and that there was 'another side to the story', which he would reveal in her defence.

Let me tell you, I couldn't wait to hear what the other side to the story was going to be. She'd already come across as such a liar, I suspected she would say anything to try to save her own skin. I would find out soon enough.

chapter 14

GUILTY

At the end of the trial, Natalie took the witness stand. It doesn't seem fair to me that it happens in that order – that the person who committed the crime is the last to take the stand before judgement. I went into my testimony blind. Natalie and her defence team got to hear all the evidence and that allowed her, frustratingly, to change her story time and time again.

Giving testimony and being cross-examined had been extremely hard on me. It forced me to relive everything, and the memories, coupled with the strange, detached environment of the courtroom, made the whole thing that much more difficult; cruel, even. I've spoken to so many victims of violent crimes who have taken the stand only to be made to feel like they're the one on trial. It doesn't seem fair to me. Natalie had all the time in the world to hear the case against her and then craft the best possible counterattack.

Even though I'd been given a clue to what was coming by the angle her lawyer had taken when cross-examining me, Natalie's defence was still unbelievably offensive. She claimed that she set me on fire in self-defence. My jaw would have hit the floor if my face hadn't been too badly scarred for me to open my mouth fully. According to her she never intended to hurt or injure me, that she acted to protect herself when I threatened her with pepper spray. In her version of events, she picked up the nearest object and threw it out of reflex – it was just bad luck that the nearest object happened to be a bottle of methylated spirits. It was even worse luck that I was holding a naked flame.

'She turned around and grabbed pepper spray,' she said. 'I immediately picked up the first thing in front of me and threw it at Dana . . . She instantly seemed to light up. I panicked.' She cried on the stand as she turned to the jury and told them she never intended to hurt me. That she'd fled the scene because she was scared, flipping out over what she'd done. She described staying home for days afterwards, getting high with her daughter in the house. 'I was numbing myself, watching the news, praying to God that she'd wake up.'

That made me sick. I imagined her sitting at home while I lay in hospital fighting for my life, her comfy on the couch with her ice pipe, watching the news and hoping against hope that I would never wake up – that I would never be able to testify against her. And now she was acting like she'd been hoping I'd survive. That was a rank display of evil. When she was asked why she'd tried to skip the country, why she'd lied to the police when she'd been arrested on suspicion of attempted murder, she replied with what was probably the only true thing she said during the whole trial: 'I lied because I was scared.' *Yeah, scared of getting caught*, I thought.

My dad, in the back of the courtroom, cried out in outrage. Later he'd tell me that he'd wanted to leap out of his seat and take matters into his own hands, full old-school Eastern European style. He's a man who migrated to the other side of the world to give his kids a better life, to protect them from the looming civil war in the former Yugoslavia, and here he was, forced to sit in silence while the woman who'd nearly killed his daughter tried to weasel out of it. No wonder he was so upset. The judge quieted the courtroom, and then the cross-examination of Natalie Dimitrovksa began.

Her story was very different to the one she'd originally given the police. While at first she'd said she'd never visited my house on the night of the attack, now she was claiming we'd gotten into an argument over her husband while getting high together, that it had gotten out of hand and that I attacked her. She denied laughing at me as she ran out of the apartment, but accepted that instead of helping she left in 'panic' and 'shock'.

At one point her lawyer conceded that his client was a 'gutless coward' and that fleeing was 'morally reprehensible'. But, he said, she was not on trial for cowardice.

That much was true. She was on trial for grievous bodily harm with intent, after lying about it to the police again and again. She got caught lying so many times; contradicting herself, changing her statement. The judge calmly addressed every sentence out of her mouth in turn and determined most of them to be flagrant lies.

Even worse was her barefaced emotional manipulation, turning on the tears for the jury. This was one moment I'll never forget. She was on the stand and she turned to the jury – not to me, not to the judge: the jury – and her eyes filled with tears and she sobbed, 'I'm gonna have to live with this for the rest of my life.'

She was talking about watching me burn alive. About how it had affected her. How *she* was going to have to live with it.

In court you are supposed to be calm and civilised – if you cause a scene it can become the basis for an appeal further down the track. If you're really disruptive you can be kicked out of the courtroom completely. I knew that, but even with it in my mind, I was seconds away from standing up and screaming at the top of my lungs: 'Are. You. For. Real? Are you serious? *You're* going to have to live with this for the rest of *your* life?'

For once I was grateful for my little T-rex arms, else I would have ripped off my mask and screamed. 'What is going on in your head? What? I have these scars for the rest of my life because you are batshit fucking crazy and violent, and you're asking us to feel sorry for you? Get a grip!' But that would have been beneath the dignity of the court, and I didn't want there to be any chance of the case being thrown out. So instead I sat and fumed behind my mask as Natalie wept her crocodile tears. No shame in her game.

I started to worry that this performance might have some effect on the jury, or the judge. I knew she was lying because I was there when she burnt me alive, but fear started to creep into me. What if they bought into the show she was putting on? Towards the end of the trial, her lawyer, faced with the mounting evidence of Natalie's guilt, had been trying to turn the narrative into one where the jury would take pity on Natalie. He tried to flip the script to paint her as a victim of circumstance. That she was damaged by an unhappy childhood and adolescence spent shifting between Macedonia, Sydney and Perth. He suggested that she was victim of a psychologically violent relationship with her estranged husband Edin. The portrait he painted was one of a woman pushed to extremes and driven to bad drugs, bad men and bad situations by the cards life had dealt her. That she was a mother, with a tiny baby girl at home who needed her.

All of that might have been true. But it didn't mean that she wasn't a liar, as well as a dangerous and violent woman. I wasn't the only person she'd hurt. Apart from all the women she'd threatened to stab over her husband, it seems she'd actually gone one step further and allegedly stabbed her husband.

It was alleged in the newspapers that, a month before she'd burnt me, she'd turned up at the unit she and Edin had shared before their separation and got into a fight with him about who would keep the furniture. At this point they'd been married for a year and they'd just had a little baby daughter together. As the fight escalated she produced a 20-centimetre Stanley knife, went into the master bedroom and began stabbing and ripping their mattress. When Edin told her to stop, she turned and stabbed him in his left shoulder, leaving a 4-centimetre gash that required two stitches. Edin called the cops and had her arrested. But she was found not guilty in court – which only goes to show how very skilled she was at escaping the consequences of her actions.

This kind of extreme behaviour seems crazy, and it's probably something most people would never understand, but in the world of illegal drugs, it's all too common. Both her and Edin seemed to have a lot of problems with methamphetamine. It wasn't long after they reconciled that they separated again and he was in court trying to have Natalie locked up – but by then I was already another victim of her violence. In any case, she slipped through the cracks in the justice system and was out on the street, free to keep committing violence.

I knew all this, but the jury did not. Because of the right to a fair trial enshrined in our legal system, her previous brushes with the law were not admissible in court. If I'd stood up and yelled, 'She stabbed the dude she burnt me alive over!' then it would have thrown the whole trial out the window. So, while Natalie lied through her teeth, I had to hold my tongue. I just had to trust that the jury would see through her act.

Finally, it was over. My friends and family moved upstairs to wait for the jury to deliver their verdict.

I wanted to have faith in the legal system, to believe that the overwhelming evidence stacked against Natalie would be enough to deliver the justice she deserved. It was hard, though. When you're in the courtroom, face to face with the person who ruined your life – and when she gets to sit there staring daggers at you while her lawyer humiliates you in front of the jury – it's hard not to let doubt overcome you.

To make it worse, on the day of the verdict, her accomplice, Daniel Stone, had turned up to court. I couldn't believe it – I was shuffling into court, on the arms of my lawyer and sister, and I looked up to see the man who watched me burnt alive just sitting there. He caught my eye, a grin broke out over his face, and then he winked at me. That was chilling – it was exactly the same wink he'd given me in my apartment on the night of the attack, as he played with Killer and idly threatened me. It was a gesture I understood perfectly. It was as if he was saying, 'Look.

I won. Whatever happens today, I got away with it.' That was almost too much for me – he'd somehow managed to avoid being charged with anything, but there he was, for no reason I could see except to gloat, to show off that he'd walked away from the whole crazy incident scot-free. To me, that's a strong indicator that he has no remorse, that he's a true psychopath.

People have often asked me why Daniel Stone wasn't charged and convicted as well, why he wasn't in that courtroom to be tried alongside Natalie, and honestly, I can think of no good reason. Now, I never once said he actually doused me in methylated spirits but he still entered my apartment unwelcomed and uninvited through the back by climbing over a wall. He could have stopped her from assaulting me, but instead he egged Natalie on and encouraged her. The man laughed while I burnt alive, then fled like a coward when I desperately needed medical help. And as far as I know, he simply got away with it. I know there are a lot of people who would like to see him charged for something. To have simply never been charged at all is beyond belief and quite shocking. I've got friends who have been charged with littering and peeing on a wall but Daniel Stone is still free. I could only hope that the justice system, despite all its flaws, would at least deliver justice to one of my assailants.

The proceedings began. The jury went out to reach a verdict. An hour passed. Two. Three.

After three and a half hours of deliberation, the jury emerged to deliver the verdict.

Guilty.

My hands clenched in shock, and I pulled them as close to my chest as I could while my family and friends crowded around and hugged me. Over in the dock, Natalie stayed cold as ice as the decision was read. For my part, I was flooded with sheer relief.

Ever since the moment I'd recovered enough from my burn to think clearly, I'd been dreading this trial. The sheer anxiety of the idea that Natalie might walk free – that she'd find the right lawyer, or judge, or get lucky, or find some way to escape justice – had been like the soundtrack of a horror movie, just humming along under every single thing I did, every single day. As long as there was the possibility of her being out on the streets, as long as this erratic and unstable woman was free to commit violence, I would always worry about the safety of myself and others. When the jury read out their decision, all that evaporated.

Outside on the court steps, the media were even more full-on than usual. Svetlana calmed them down and then she spoke for us. 'Thank you to all of the people who have supported Dana and our family,' she said. 'Today's verdict brought us a lot of relief. The trial was nothing when you have to sit there and dress somebody and cover their wounds every morning. What's become normal for my mum and myself, it's unbearable. Sitting through the trial was nothing, the hardest part was seeing her [Natalie].'

Svetlana took a few moments to thank everyone who had offered kind wishes, acknowledging the tens of thousands of messages from strangers that had arrived wishing me well in the past year and a half. When someone asked how we felt about the guilty verdict she was direct. 'We couldn't be happier, and look forward to her getting a lengthy sentence.'

As far as I was concerned it couldn't be lengthy enough. Natalie was looking at a maximum of twenty years, but I thought they should throw away the key. I would be facing surgery and living with scars for the rest of my days. The sentence she gave me is for life – surely at the very least she deserves the same. As long as she was behind bars, she wouldn't be able to ruin anybody else's life the way she had mine.

Sentencing wouldn't be until couple of months later. While my mind could rest a little easier then, there would still be no rest for me physically. My treatment wasn't going to wait. I'd delayed having important operations so that I was free for the trial but now I had to get straight back into it. The trial finished on a Wednesday and that Friday I was going under general anaesthetic for surgery. Now that my attacker was remanded in custody, the real battle could continue.

chapter 15

SENTENCING

The sentencing was held on 11 October 2013. That was when I would finally feel free from the courts, from the anxiety that came from the trial, from further harm. I would discover how long my attacker would be in prison for. For the three months since the trial, I'd been living in a kind of fog – seeing my doctors, doing my exercises, working on my recovery, but it was like there was a cloud hanging over me. I knew, logically, that I was safe from harm, that Natalie was behind bars. But when you've been the victim of a criminal assault, it can be hard to believe in your heart that you are free.

She was already in prison, waiting for sentencing, but the amount of time she would ultimately spend inside depended on the discretion of the judge. She could potentially be behind bars for decades or be out in a few years – an idea that horrified me. The judge could give her a maximum of twenty years' imprisonment, but in the history of Perth's legal system there had never been a punishment that severe. It could be much more lenient. The severity of the assault was unprecedented, so there was nothing that it could be compared to that might give me an idea of what might happen.

When I turned up to court on the day of the sentencing, the usual media scrum was waiting. My family pushed through and we found our seats. The air was tense. After opening proceedings, Judge Bruce Goetze got straight down to business.

'All right. Ms Dimitrovska, you can remain seated,' he said, before briefly touching on the assault and the charges she'd stood trial for: namely to 'maim, disfigure, disable or do some grievous bodily harm to Dana Vulin.' The judge noted that she'd pled not guilty and that the jury had decided otherwise.

He gave a summary of the facts: that she was separated from her husband, that she'd made many threatening phone calls to me, one after another, saying things like 'You're dead, bitch', 'I'll ruin your pretty little face' and 'We're watching you'. In his careful, measured speech, the judge repeated back much of the abuse that Natalie had sent my way, including that she hoped I would be 'raped, beaten and murdered'.

The judge went through all the facts in excruciating detail – the threats, the stalking, the first visit to my apartment, the escalating death threats. Through it all, Natalie sat impassive, staring ahead, cold as you like, until finally the judge recounted the attack.

'On 15 February you were smoking amphetamine. You did so throughout the night and into the early hours of the morning on 16 February. After sunrise you went to Ms Vulin's apartment,' Judge Goetze said. Then he recounted the attack, both my version – with her waving the bottle back and forth – and hers, in which she threw the first object that she found at me in self-defence. He noted that the expert witnesses had said that, by the pattern of damage the fire had caused, this was impossible. He warned her sternly, 'By that defence you sought to lay blame on Ms Vulin and that does you no credit.'

At that moment, a mobile phone rang, breaking the intensity of the moment. The judge looked up, annoyed, and asked the owner of the phone to leave the court. He then turned back to Natalie without missing a beat.

'Now, it's really difficult to imagine how one human being could leave while another human being was on fire. Your laughter at Ms Vulin was both cruel and derisive. You failed to provide her with assistance which could have rendered her injuries far less severe than those with which she has ended up. It's totally unimaginable how you could not have helped to put out the flames or try to do so, or at least call for help. Instead, as I say, you laughed and ran away.'

Judge Goetze paused for a second to let this sink in, then continued, recounting how she had driven away from the scene, warning Jessica Mazza, who had been sitting in the car, 'Do not to say anything about this to anyone.' He then reminded Natalie that she had been heard on police phone taps discussing changing her hair colour to avoid detection, and how she was then busted trying to flee the country. 'My finding is, consistent with the evidence and the verdict of the jury, that the attempt to flee from Australia was solely because of a consciousness of guilt in respect of the offending for which you've now been committed.'

Then he turned to evidence from my surgeons, about the damage done to me, the operations I'd already had, the fact that I would require dozens more in the future. That my injuries would require daily medical treatment for years, if not the rest of my life, and had caused permanent physical and psychological trauma. 'The challenges she faces will be lifelong.'

He noted that I had to learn to walk again, that I still hadn't even showered or dressed myself in nineteen months, that I couldn't raise my hands in the air. 'And,' the judge observed, 'I suppose Ms Vulin cannot even brush her hair or put on some makeup.'

Too true. I didn't expect the judge to sympathise with my cosmetics crisis, but I hadn't put on makeup in all that time – and I love makeup. In my opinion, a woman's right to wear mascara should basically be protected by law. I used to wear so much of it that, when I was first burnt, the first thing that Svet noticed about me was my mascara.

My eyebrows were burnt right off, but not my eyelashes. They were intact because I was wearing so much mascara. They took the bullet for me. After that, just try to tell me that mascara isn't a basic human right.

The judge said that somebody who hadn't suffered my injuries couldn't really understand the suffering, but concluded this:

'You have totally ruined Ms Vulin's life . . . She is a person who had potential and you have deprived her of using that potential. You have also deprived her immediate family of the joy that would have come from her being successful, both at work and, at twenty-seven, you might reasonably expect her to have married and had a family.

'So the impact of your offending cannot truly be understood by anyone other than Ms Vulin and those very close to her. She had much to look forward to in life; she must have a strong will for life and a steel grit and determination to have seen herself through a very traumatic time.'

The judge was just getting warmed up, talking about how Natalie now had something I never would. She would finish her sentence and one day be able to leave prison, and could look forward to spending time with her daughter again. That was something she had taken away from me. He mentioned that my health had been destroyed to the point where not only was I crippled, it was a possibility I would never be able to have children. To illustrate, he produced the victim impact statement I'd written for

the court. For Natalie's benefit, to help her truly understand what she had done, he read it in full.

I am living hell on earth. I still wake up every day
thinking, hoping, this is all a dream. How quickly I am
reminded the moment I go to move and am in pain.
The moment I look down and see a burns garment,
and worst of all the moment I look down to see and
feel my body riddled in scars – scars so bad and so ugly
you could only think to see them in a nightmare. The
nightmare I have lived, am living, and will live for the
rest of my life.

To be able to explain to anyone, I mean really
explain, how painful it was being set on fire, is really,
truly impossible. There are no words, but as painful and
scary as being set on fire is, the aftermath is a billion
times worse. It is even hard to explain the look people
give when they see me, the pity and sadness they feel
for me and give me, the shock they have when they
see me – and how scared children get by my physical
appearance. That is something I am going to get for the
rest of my life, something I don't think I could ever get
used to.

Where to begin? How do you put into words that
you have literally lost everything and then some?
That you have been stripped as a person of everything,
from the physical right down to your very soul. The day
I was set on fire, not only did my body get burnt but my

mind was burnt, my passions and desires got burnt, my love for life, self-confidence and sexuality – all burnt. My hopes, dreams and future ambitions all burnt. My family and the people around me also so badly burnt and severely scarred, mentally and permanently.

I'm supposed to be in the prime of my life, but I'm not. It is passing me by and I am missing everything, every special event, engagements, birthdays, and even funerals. I want more than anything just to be normal again, to have the skin I was born with, the skin my parents gave me. I would love to dress myself just one time, or tie my hair in a simple ponytail, but I can't and won't ever have my skin back no matter how hard or how many tears I cry.

There are times where I have cried so hard it felt like my eyes were bleeding, times where I have been so sad it felt like my soul was broken and I simply couldn't move, not even to physically hold myself up, my body so weak from sadness.

I cannot count how many nights' sleep I've lost from pure sadness, physical pain and an uncontrollable itch, an itch that hasn't stopped, not once, not even for a day, not even for an hour, with no end in sight. Even now as I write this I'm itchy and I'm in pain in more than one place at a time.

My mum and sister have become my legs, my arms, my carers, my providers, my physios, my occupational therapists, my physical strength, my drivers, my groomers, my dressers, my nurses, and I have become their life, living and breathing for my recovery, which is a full-time job for them both together.

Even though they both constantly claim they are happy to do it and would have it no other way, I still constantly feel like a huge burden and I hate it. I used to be an independent outgoing woman and now I can barely do anything for myself.

I constantly think about how hard and exhausting it is emotionally and physically on my mother and sister and how much better I think their lives would be if I wasn't burnt. It makes me feel like I'm ruining their lives, which kills me. I feel like a burden and it plays on my emotions big time.

Basically adding insult to injury, even though they still always constantly reassure me I'm not, I just feel that this should have been my problem only and they are such beautiful, amazing people who I truly believe deserve the best, happy lives and I hate that their lives have been affected so much and ceased because of this.

To try and come to terms that this has happened to me is a challenge within itself. Maybe it would be easier to do if it was a freak accident or I did it to myself. But the fact that somebody intentionally set me on fire to eradicate my appearance, someone I did nothing to, is something I will never come to terms with or be able to understand.

I have lost the feeling of freedom and the feeling of being safe. I don't feel safe any more, anywhere, even in my own home. I'm constantly checking the locks and worried about security and it's causing me more anxiety.

I can't tell you what it's like, even now, nineteen months later. Imagine not being able to shower and dress yourself and having to ask for assistance for everything. Imagine even the simplest of tasks, like not being able to reach up and grab a glass. Imagine supposedly being in the prime of your life and not going anywhere, not a single place.

Imagine having to wear the same compression garment and horrible faceless mask for two years. Imagine having to be massaged three times daily with creams to help soften the skin, especially while the scars are still active and hypersensitive.

Imagine having open wounds for nineteen months so far, with no end in sight. Imagine constant excruciating pain and knowing you have a lifetime of surgeries to face. Imagine physio every single day, only to be so debilitated and limited.

Imagine having to look in the mirror or down at your body and absolutely hating what you see, and then imagine knowing someone else did this to you on purpose because of your appearance.

Finally, imagine the possibility of not being able to have children because of this person. Well, I don't have to imagine this because this is my horrible, grim and sad reality. I will have a lifetime of permanent physical, psychological and functionality problems. I am serving the hardest, worst life sentence a person can serve.

After he read the statement, Judge Goetze put down his papers and let the words sink in. He then turned back to Natalie and started to speak about mitigating factors – all the things that had gone wrong in her life for her to end up in court for ruining someone else's. He said he was taking into account that she'd left school at sixteen, and had spent a decade moving to new cities in Macedonia, New South Wales and Western Australia, getting into harder and harder drugs through the years: cannabis, heroin and, finally, crystal meth.

The judge took into consideration her estrangement from her husband, the psychologically violent nature of her marriage, as well as the anti-social drug-dealing, drug-taking world that she belonged to, and had since she was a teenager. The judge understood that in that world, the values and expectations of people can be warped, and she was playing by a different set of rules.

The judge also took into account that Natalie had a daughter only two years old, and it had to be noted that an extended prison sentence was going to deprive the little girl of her mother. At this point, Natalie started to lose her composure and, despite myself, I almost felt sorry for her. She'd turned me into a human fireball, derailed my existence, destroyed my body and face, my life, tried to murder me – but I pictured that poor little girl growing up without her mother around. And then later becoming aware of why she wasn't there, what Natalie had done to make it so she would spend her daughter's best years locked away.

It was such a sad thought that, in a moment of panic, I began to be filled with dread at the possibility that the judge had too much sympathy for her. What if Natalie's sad life was enough for him to decide to go easy on her?

I didn't have to worry, though. The judge soon moved on to Natalie's evaluation by a psychologist, who testified that she was focused on her own needs, which, in combination with her personality type, explained her notable lack of empathy.

He noted that drugs alone could not explain why she didn't help after burning me. Nor her 'distorted perception' that she too was a victim. It was clear from her testimony that if she had any remorse about attacking me, it came only from having been caught and punished. She simply didn't seem to understand that the suffering she had caused me was worse than hers.

'You grieve for the loss of your life and not being with your daughter . . . You see yourself as – and I quote – "the girl who burnt the other girl. I will never be the same". . . I received a letter from you expressing sorrow for Ms Vulin, and that's expressed really in one paragraph, basically one line. The rest of the letter is all about you and the situation you find yourself in.'

That moment was extremely satisfying. That's when I realised that my worst fears would not come true, that in trying – unbelievably – to paint herself as the victim, Natalie had dug her own grave. The judge had seen through her manipulation. 'What [the psychologist] Ms Fowler says is that you look at matters from the point of view of impact upon you. And that's really how your letter to me reads.'

The judge had considered all the mitigating factors and decided they weren't enough.

'Failing to help Ms Vulin was cowardly. But any remorse that you feel is really you now feeling sorry for yourself in the position which you're in, rather than having genuine remorse for your actions and empathy with Ms Vulin.

'You intentionally caused her grievous bodily harm resulting in very serious physical and psychological injuries. These injuries impact every minute in her life in the manner she's described in the victim impact statement.

'Her injuries will impact upon every interaction she has with another human being for the rest of her life. Her immediate family and friends may well become used to her situation. They will have to provide round-the-clock care for her. But any other person she meets will, trying as best they can to not show some reaction, recoil in some way or have some reaction and Ms Vulin will feel that. She has no chance of ever leading a normal life again. This has to be a worst category case.'

The judge concluded that this crime was the worst of its sort, and the worst punishment would have to be delivered. He announced that Natalie Dimitrovska would serve seventeen years in prison, with a minimum of fifteen. It was the longest and most severe sentence handed down for grievous bodily harm in Perth's history. An unprecedented punishment for an unprecedented crime.

Hearing that made me feel so validated, especially as the judge went into detail as to why she was receiving that sentence. I was just so happy that, after so long dealing with murky half-truths and wild media speculation, and then the trial and Natalie's feeble excuses, my truth had finally been tested and confirmed. The judge had calmly dissected the case, weighed up every piece of evidence, and delivered a sentence that was perfectly fair.

As the sentence was read out, Natalie burst into tears. So did I. But mine were uncontrollable happy tears. I really hadn't thought the justice system would get it right, but the judge was so thorough. In examining the crime and what it had done to me and my family, he touched on every single important issue.

For two and a half years I had been holding my breath, unable to move on with my life because this trial had been hanging over me. But in the end everyone – from the police to the prosecution to the judge – did an immaculate job. Thanks to them, I could finally exhale.

The next night, we went to see Ricky Martin for Svet's birthday. That was the perfect bookend to the whole three-month ordeal of the trial. The night before the trial had started, I'd been so destroyed by anticipation that I'd fallen asleep in my seat, watching *Disney On Ice*. Now, watching Ricky bump and grind through his set, with everyone in the crowd getting down, even some old grannies, I could finally relax. I had the rest of my life ahead of me, and I had my family. And now that the trial was over, I was free to do whatever I dreamt. My assailant was in chains, but mine were only just coming off, and I was going to make the most of it.

chapter 16

REMOVING THE MASK

It's impossible to overstate how important the verdict was to me. It meant I was safe – that I could finally blow away the dark cloud that had been hanging over me since the moment I'd woken from my coma. At times, when my morale was low, when I was trapped in my hospital bed, strapped into the crucifix with nothing to do but stare at the ceiling, my thoughts would betray me and I would think about Natalie, and how she had put me in hospital. Now that she was behind bars for nearly two decades, I could finally let that go.

The sense of relief was overwhelming. And it meant I was finally free to tell my story.

Up until the sentencing, I'd been silent out of respect for the rules of the law. From the moment I'd regained consciousness after the attack, the police had warned me about the importance of not talking to anyone but them and my lawyers about what had happened. If any information got out and was reported in the media, it could prejudice the jury and cause a mistrial. If the trial was aborted, or even abandoned, because of something I'd let slip to the media, that would be catastrophic. Worse, it would be my fault. So, when the media came knocking, I bit my tongue, stayed silent, and hoped that the legal system would find the truth.

It wasn't always easy staying silent. Everyone seemed to want to know my story. While I was still in the coma, my Facebook page was flooded with messages of support from people who wanted to know how they could help or who were asking how I was doing. Svet made an announcement on her own Facebook account: 'We will not let this despicable act break the contagious "conquer everything" attitude to life Dana is best known for.' That helped our loved ones, but couldn't hope to reach the thousands of strangers who were reaching out to us. The support just kept coming in; first a trickle, then a flood, of positive messages. So a longtime friend of mine, Yasmin, made a public Facebook page where people could come and check in, and support me and each other. It started with a simple message on 17 February 2012:

'There are no words to describe the pain that the Vulin family and friends are going through. We love Dana dearly and are here to support her and her family. Please show your support, wishes, photos and happy memories you have with the amazing Dana Vulin. She is such a strong woman. We know she will pull through this!'

That's how it all started. Within days, thousands of complete strangers had joined the page. They must have found me after news reports of the attack appeared on websites across the world. The messages came pouring in. There were literally thousands of messages from strangers all over the world who wanted to offer their sympathy or to ask if there was anything they could do to help.

While I was still in the coma, Svet sat by my bedside, reading out the messages. She had no way of knowing if they were getting through to me, but she thought that if I could hear and understand her, then knowing there was a whole world out there praying for my survival could only help. And it did, it really did.

And after I regained consciousness, those messages were a huge source of comfort early on. They helped me to recover from the shock and cruelty of my attack, to know that there were so many good people out there in the world. Even the simplest of messages: 'Stay strong. We're thinking of you.' They made all the difference.

I was blessed to have a community of well-wishers there for me from day one after my attack, connecting with me through social media and through newspapers, radio and television. Sometimes the media attention was a bit of a blessing, like those first, vital messages of support that reached my hospital bed in the heart of the ICU. And all the people who called Crime Stoppers to inform on

Natalie after Svetlana and the police appealed for information through the media. Without them, there's every chance Natalie would have escaped to Macedonia and never been captured and punished.

But for every bit of good that part of the media did, sometimes they made the whole situation a hundred times more difficult. They wrote whatever they wanted about me, and for over a year and a half I didn't have a voice. I maintained a dignified silence as the media picked over what was left of my old life and trashed my privacy.

Now, though, I was free to finally tell my side of things, to find my voice. I could take control of my story, my life and my destiny.

Since the trial had ended and the gag order on talking about my experiences had been lifted, the media attention had doubled, and then doubled again. Everyone was hounding me for an exclusive on the story, but my family and I had thought about this for a long time, and knew that we had to do it right. Part of me wanted to just tell the story in a low-key way, reaching out to the community that had built up around the Facebook page, but we knew we needed to go bigger than that if we were going to do the right thing. I wanted to get the truth out there, to cut through all the lies and the nonsense. My experience had taught me how very lonely a victim of crime can feel, and how powerless in the face of the system. I figured that if I could show the world not only the truth but that I had come through my challenges with my heart undiminished, then I could make a difference to any other survivors of crime going through a hard time.

Two things had restrained me from showing any of my personality to the world since the day of the burn. The first were the legal restrictions that had robbed me of my voice; the second was the pressure mask that had robbed me of my face. By now, nearly three years had passed since the burn, and my doctors had given me the all clear. I was ready to show my face to the world. The court-ordered silence I'd been forced to hide behind had been removed, and now, so too would the mask.

I made my media debut on *Sunday Night*, the current affairs show, with a two-part television special. The first episode would air right after the sentencing, where I would tell my story about the attack and my life as a burns survivor. The second episode would air nearly a year later, in which I would show my face to the world without my mask for the first time. This was a big deal to me. Nobody except my family and my medical team had seen my face since the burn. I'd fought hard to make sure the paparazzi never saw me without my mask on, and again in the courtroom when the prosecution tried to make me appear without it. It was a huge and difficult decision to make, but in the end I agreed to appear on the show and to debut my burns to the world.

The thing that tipped me over into making the decision to share my story was the memory of those first, hopeless months after my injury, when I'd searched everywhere on the internet for information, especially before and after photos of burn survivors, and was never able to find the hope I needed. I knew that if someone else had shared their story, if I'd been able to find that frame of reference and the hope that came with it, my recovery would have been so much easier.

The silver lining to everything I'd been through, was the wealth of experience I could now share. Now I knew what worked, what didn't, how to find hope when everything is hopeless – and that's something that every survivor deserves access to. So, in a way, the decision to appear on television was out of my hands. I thought I had a responsibility to put a face – my face – on burns survival. To show what we are capable of.

I made all this clear to the producers. If I was going to appear on their show, if I was going to remove my mask, I wanted it to be as a survivor, not as a victim. Someone who was proud of her achievements in recovery, strengthened by the burn rather than diminished. They agreed, and so filming started. They interviewed me, my mum, my neighbour Denis, who'd rescued me, my surgeon Professor Rea, the police officers who caught and prosecuted Natalie – everyone and anyone who could help tell the real story behind my burns.

The story was filmed as a TV special called *The Girl Behind the Mask*. It was told in two parts: an initial segment where they talked about the attack and my recovery and a follow-up television special where they covered the trial.

At the climax of the show, I would remove my mask and show my face and body, scars and all, to the world for the first time.

If you've seen the footage of me taking off the mask, that was for real. That was the first time I'd removed the mask in front of anyone but my closest circle. I was nervous about it, but the producers insisted they wanted me to take my mask off in front of Australia, and by that point, so did I. We wanted the authenticity, but I was worried that my face wasn't really ready to show the world. I discussed my doubts with the producers, but also my desire to demonstrate what was possible in burns recovery and to show how far somebody could come. I'd taken so much inspiration from Caroline Mayer and those like her who were brave enough to face the world, even after losing nearly everything – and I had something unique to share with the world, something that could provide comfort to other survivors out there.

And yet, I could have worn my mask a little longer. The mask was an important part of my physical recovery, smoothing and healing my skin, but it also had a psychological effect. It was so much a part of the identity I showed to the world that I had come to rely on it. I've spoken to a lot of other survivors who have worn a mask and they've told me a similar story. It really does become a comfort thing – like insulation between me and the world. Of course, as much as I respected the mask, the day the doctors told me I didn't have to wear it any more, I was like *zip, zip,* off you go, catch you later, Mr Mask. I'm happy to never have to put it on again. But I did keep it, just in case, the way you might keep a security blanket from childhood that you'll never actually use again. At that point, the mask felt like a part of me.

Before the *Sunday Night* story aired, I had mixed emotions. Excited, definitely, but also extremely nervous. They'd filmed over a hundred hours of footage altogether, from all aspects of my life. For days on end a camera crew followed me everywhere, filming every minute detail of my day-to-day existence.

They filmed me doing physiotherapy, going through remedial exercises, boxing with a punching bag. There were personal moments; fun, chill ones, just hanging out with my family, including me at a children's birthday party, dancing with some children with my wonky little arms, jumping up and down on a bouncy castle. There were also very private moments of me in pain, undergoing massage, climbing into my pressure garment and swearing like a sailor. I had no way to know what footage they would be using in the broadcast.

My one-on-one interview with reporter Rahni Sadler was wide-ranging and touched on some difficult topics, but I wasn't about to shy away from them. I'd walked through hell and I wasn't afraid to face what I'd been through. Other times, I felt a little bit embarrassed about being filmed – like in my boxing class, when my top slipped down and I accidentally gave everyone a bit of an eyeful. I couldn't even reach up to cover myself because of my limited mobility. My arm just didn't bend that way, so I had to wait until a producer stepped in and pulled my top up for me. It was a little bit mortifying, but nothing I wasn't used to. I'd come too far to get embarrassed by some little thing like that.

But then there was the incident with the Cher song.

They wanted some footage of me doing all the stuff I'd fought so hard to be able to do: walk around, dress myself, make a sandwich, the simple things. That included footage of me driving my car, to show how far I'd come in my recovery. I'd only recently got my new licence, after having to sit the test again and prove I was capable with my new injuries. Having my own car meant I was free to drive myself around, and to and from hospital every day – a wonderful feeling after being so utterly dependent on others for years. The producers wanted to capture that feeling of elation, so they put a camera in the car. It was all going well, until this Cher song, 'You Haven't Seen the Last of Me', came on the radio. Now, I really loved that song, it's all about being unbroken and strong and rising up from being knocked down. I started singing along without thinking about the camera – or the fact that I'm not what you'd call a great singer. But I didn't worry about them using the footage; the audience was there to be confronted by my burns, not my voice.

Most of all, I loved *Sunday Night*'s idea for how I would reveal my face to the world, which was to have me walk out at a fashion show, all glammed up in a designer dress. I wanted to do it in a way that was true to my Dana-ness, something that would show that I was proud of who I am and of my body. My new body, that is, my post-burn body. The one that I'd fought to reclaim from the burn and the scars. I wanted to show that I had the confidence to walk alongside any other woman, even if it meant walking the catwalk with professional models. We hit on the idea of filming the reveal at a real fashion show, a showcase of next season's formal wear. A bunch of other models would go first, showing off the dresses, and then I would close the show.

On the day I was the last to come up on stage. The lights went dim and I walked out on the catwalk in this beautiful black Betty Tran gown. When I got to the end of the platform the lights went up, and the cameras caught my face for all the world to see.

It was nice, although it felt a bit OTT, with the big dramatic reveal, the extravagant hair and makeup, but I still owned it as much as I could. It was a wonderful moment, and so healing for me – the girl who'd been burnt by a madwoman, who'd crawled back from death's door, walking down the runway of a real-life fashion show in a beautiful gown, turning and seeing all my family and best friends there in the front row, cheering me on.

I'd been a little bit nervous about people – dudes from the film crew, total strangers – seeing my face after years behind the mask. My closest family and friends had seen my new face, carefully rebuilt with dozens of surgeries and years of painful exercise and physiotherapy, but I knew I didn't look like the girl I'd once been. That's a massive psychological hurdle to overcome, but it was actually so easy. Everyone was super chill and kind, and, best of all, the barrier between me and the world was finally gone. For years, I'd been unable to express myself with my face. If I was smiling, or frowning, or giving someone a dirty look, they had no idea. That's a very alienating experience and so, when I took off my mask and smiled, everyone in the room knew exactly how I felt.

As the first episode of the two-part special went to air, I was acutely aware that all around Australia, millions of total strangers were about to have a window into my most private self. It was an intense and surreal feeling, but not a bad one.

Overall, I was very happy with the show. Except for the singing, of course. They didn't have to run the video of me singing. That was unforgivable! They ran it in full, just me tootling down the highway in my mask, howling along. Oh man. They had a hundred hours of footage – I have no idea why they used that little bit of it! By then, I was mentally strong enough to show Australia my scars, but I don't think I'll ever be ready for the world to hear my singing.

And then they did it again! When they ran the second episode they ran the footage of me singing again. Because it aired on the east coast first, my girlfriends in Melbourne and Sydney saw it three hours before me. They were messaging me and paying me out about my singing, and I thought they were winding me up. I figured there was no way they'd run the footage again. I couldn't believe it – I got fully shamed. *Twice!* All I could do was laugh.

By the time the mask came off and the whole of Australia saw my face, I was like, '*Really, after hearing me sing, this kind of exposure is no big deal.*'

But you know what? It was a big deal. It was huge. Finally having a voice to tell my story was so liberating and I felt like I'd got a big burden off my shoulders. It was hard, I was scared, but it was worth it.

My story must have really touched a nerve out there. In the first week after sharing my story with Australia, I had 1.6 million people visit my *We Heart Dana Vulin* Facebook page and by the second week that number had reached 2.5 million. Until then, I'd never really comprehended how valuable my story might be. People from all over the world, all walks of life, reached out to let me know that they were also going through some heavy shit, and seeing me power through mine gave them hope. It blew my mind how much my story had not only moved people but affected their lives. Sure, my scars might not be my favourite thing to look at, but I was so touched when total strangers looked at my scars and, instead of horror, they saw hope. I was surprised by the level of love that's out there. It made me glad that I did the interview, knowing that I could help so many people.

I was so moved that I wrote a letter to the audience of *Sunday Night* to let them know how grateful I was for their well-wishing.

Where to even start? What happened to me was so evil and so heinous, but it took something so ugly, so cruel and so bad to see so much beauty, love and good.

This experience has made it clearly evident to me that there are so many more good, kind-hearted people out there than there are bad. Words will never be able to truly and thoroughly express the gratitude and appreciation I feel towards every person, everywhere who has supported me in one way or another.

The response from the public has been the best surprise ever. Since the burn and wearing the mask, my nephews have called me their superhero. When the mask comes off, I'm still going to do my best to be that hero. I would love to be able to help people and to give back the encouragement, advice, support and inspiration for those who may need it.

Total respect and gratitude, God bless!

I meant every word of that letter. The support of so many people meant the world to me. It made me realise that I'd been trusted with something really precious: the good-will of strangers. It really inspired me, pushed me to work harder, to go above and beyond. The media attention on my burn and the aftermath had never been something I'd wanted, but it was here, and I could use it to do good in the world.

chapter 17

SEEKING TREATMENT

I'd learnt pretty early on that I wasn't going to recover the way I wanted unless I went at it like a madwoman. The process is so long, and so painful. It really is an endless struggle. My time in hospital gave me every chance to recover but that was only the beginning of what I would need to get to where I wanted to be. I worked, physically and mentally, day and night on my recovery – I empowered myself and searched high and low for anything that could help.

I searched everywhere for information, hunting through every corner of the internet for the smallest hints of what would happen to me as my scars matured. Every night my sister and I would stay up researching, emailing, making calls, reading medical articles until our eyes ached with exhaustion, and I came away frustrated just about every time. I was desperate to know what therapies and treatments were available that might help me to recover more fully than the badly burnt and crippled people I was seeing in my research. In the beginning, though, I could never really find anything. It just wasn't out there.

That, more than anything else, is why I made the decision to share my story. I'd been truly desperate for something as simple as before-and-after pictures, to show me what was in store for me, but there was nothing like that. So I wanted to become that point of reference. I know what it's like to be desperate to find some hope, desperate to find answers.

Hope is everything. It changes your entire outlook on recovery. When there's nothing to give you that hope, it puts you in an impossible place. To come back from a bad burn, you need to fight harder than any human being should ever have to. How are you supposed to fight when you have no idea what you are fighting for? Of what the possibilities are? So I made myself public, made the decision to share everything: the burns, the pain, the photos – both horrible and hopeful – so that anyone out there in the world who reached out for help would be able to find it. I already had a public profile and was determined to use that platform for good. I wanted to become an advocate in the media for burns survivors, and, beyond that, anyone facing adversity.

Part of being an advocate meant being willing to try anything that gave me a chance at a better life for me and other survivors of trauma. I made a decision to go beyond the expected minimum. I didn't want to survive; I wanted to thrive. I would beat this burn.

Instead of running from the pain, I learnt to appreciate it. It meant that I was still alive, that I was getting better. I opted to have any operation or procedure, any possibility of improvement, no matter how much it hurt. Over the years, that's meant hundreds and hundreds of steroid injections, experimental creams, chemical peels. I tried this dermabrasion cream that was designed for elderly people who get skin cancer on their faces. It basically burns the top layers of skin off and, as far as I understood, produces collagen. So I went to my surgeons and said, 'Guys, theoretically, this removes skin and produces collagen, which is what we need, right? Can I try it? What have I got to lose?'

The thing is, skin is such a complex thing. It has to breathe, it has to sweat, grow, feel, touch, and when it is damaged it can be unpredictable. Sometimes, a treatment I had pinned all this hope on would just backfire completely. I've tried heaps of stuff that's failed and fucked me up worse. I tried an experimental heat treatment that completely distorted the skin on my body. Instead of diminishing the scar it just created a whole new layer of scar – scar tissue was layered over scar tissue. Another time I tried a derma treatment, which not only hurt like hell but made a huge hole in my face that didn't heal for years and years. Even now, I have a slight depression there when I run my finger over it. Every treatment that didn't work out was painful, and a little bit heartbreaking. Some of them were beyond heartbreaking. I haven't just had facial treatments fail, but skin grafts, surgical interventions, release operations. I've watched newly grafted skin fall off and die in front of my eyes, something no human being should ever have to experience. But it was all worth it. It *might* have worked, and that's what counts.

And there is stuff that works. I am living proof. Steroid injections, massage, creams, silicone treatments. It's imperative that new burns survivors know about them as soon as possible. The thing is, the burns community has such special, individual needs. Every single person really does burn, heal and scar differently, so not every treatment was going to work for me. And while there was precious little useful information on actual treatments, there's plenty of bullshit out there. If you search 'burns remedies' online there are a million and one ooga-booga remedies that claim to be the ultimate cure, some of it really far out stuff. Even my distant relatives in Serbia would come over to visit and bring all sorts of weird superstitious and traditional cures. I once read an article that suggested you can smooth out scars from third-degree burns by ironing your skin with a clothes iron. Needless to say, please do not try that at home.

And there were a lot of well-meaning companies who would suggest solutions that were just not right for me. One company offered a cream that regenerated collagen and refreshed the dermis. Svet had to write back and say, 'We appreciate what you're doing, but Dana has no dermis or epidermis so your creams won't help. Thank you, but no.' It was really hard to say no to people who genuinely wanted to help, but I had to be smart about what I tried. I was willing to try anything, but I wouldn't go into it blind.

Svetlana and I quickly became a two-woman research team. Her scientific education gave her a good understanding of how the body works; the sort of effects different medications can have on you, how different treatments might affect my injuries. She's not a doctor but she knew how to read medical journals, could translate medical jargon for me, and then mediate with the burns team at Royal Perth. That made her the perfect companion when searching for treatments. If I came across something in my research I would get Svetlana to look at it, and together we would work out whether it was an option for me. If we figured it was worth a shot, we would find a way to make it happen.

Lots of wonderful people around the world are working tirelessly to ease the suffering of burns survivors, to make their day-to-day lives a little bit easier. We looked at every option and explored a bunch of new ones, using our first-hand experience as a guide. I knew what it was like to deal with the daily agony and frustration of burns recovery and the status-quo treatments and recovery. And Svetlana knew what a back-breaking, endless sacrifice it was to care for someone in those circumstances. Together, we came at every problem with intimate knowledge of what we needed and the desire to find a path.

We trialled some treatments that were not common options in Australia when we first asked about them. And we even helped develop a few new ones because, as the one undergoing them, I had an insider's perspective of what could be done to improve on them.

For example, my compression garments were a small miracle of medicine, but they were clearly designed by somebody who'd never had to wear one over circumferential burns for three years. Wearing the garment every day, I could identify ways to improve it and take ideas for little customisations to my medical team.

Having big boobs turned out to be a bit of an issue when it came to the pressure garment. My breasts are on the larger side and (thank God!) they had survived the fire intact. But the garment wasn't designed with boobs in mind, so it wasn't helping the scar tissue across my chest. It was really serious for a while, with the scars there getting angry and raised, so I worked with my brilliant occupational therapist Rosemary Kendall to design a sternum chest strap to apply pressure to my cleavage and chest. It looked like of like a reverse bra with a bit of a bondage style to it. That just wasn't around beforehand.

Sometimes it was just a matter of joining the dots, of thinking about existing stuff in a new way. During the day I'd wear my beige compression mask, but occasionally

I would try out this other type of rigid acrylic mask. It was really tight, having been specially designed to compress certain cells to smooth out my facial scars. It was ugly as fuck, but we had the idea of incorporating silicon into my regular mask. Sometimes it just takes a new perspective to shake things up. Things like that only seem simple after they've already been done. I was the first patient in the hospital to wear a silicone-aligned acrylic mask, but definitely not the last.

Whenever I found something that had worked for me, or if I had an operation that had gone well – or even badly – I found myself sharing online; the good, the bad, and the ugly. Every day messages would ping into my email or on the *We Heart Dana Vulin* Facebook page. Often they were messages of support, but sometimes they were people looking for advice, or asking after the outcome of procedures I'd had.

Before long I had become that person I'd been looking for myself – someone people could turn to when they were scared and needed answers. Soon, not a day passed by without strangers reaching out to me for help. They came from all walks of life. Most of the time they found out about me through my media profile. Sometimes, they too had media profiles. I'd watched the reality show *Real Housewives of Melbourne* and felt the greatest empathy, as Janet Roach, one of the stars, had nearly lost her son Jake in a petrol fire. The poor boy had been only twenty-two when he suffered burns to 70 per cent of his body.

I knew exactly what he'd been through. Not long after that, he followed me on Instagram, and I followed back. Soon we were chatting and supporting each other on our journeys of recovery. When we both found ourselves in Melbourne, we ended up catching up and hanging out, exchanging treatment stories but mostly just having a laugh and talking shit.

That's the great power of social media – it lets survivors connect with each other, to provide support and knowledge, just like the burns retreats that are so important to recovery. The fact that I was able to use my profile to spread that support is such a blessing.

It also led me to connecting with one of my own heroes, the woman who I'd looked to for hope when I needed it the most. I was pretty much as excited as I'd ever been when I realised that Katie Piper – the British acid-attack victim who'd inspired me so much in the early days of my recovery – was following me on social media. I reached out to her and she responded, and soon we'd become electronic pen-pals and exchanged phone numbers. These days we share a lot of stuff with each other, and she's been there for me as a friend and mentor. Having someone supporting me who's been through what I'm going through is so very valuable, and I spend hours and hours each week responding to everybody who I can potentially play that role for.

As more and more people reached out directly to me for help with their own recovery, as well as scared family members for guidance in caring for their loved ones, I soon realised that my experience wasn't a curse. I mean, it was *awful*, but it was also a chance to do some good, to make a difference and contribute to a better world. And if I had to pick one moment when I realised we really could make a difference, it would be when we got our hands on the laser.

chapter 18

THE GOOD FIGHT

While Svetlana and I were researching procedures and techniques, we came across this new kind of therapy, the Lumenis UltraPulse fractional CO_2 laser. It was brand new technology, really cutting-edge stuff. It was also extremely rare and pricey. The American military had had great success using it to help army guys who had been hit by shrapnel and incendiary devices.

It was a relatively new invention at that time, but early reports indicated it could fast-forward a scar maturing, remodel the collagen within the scar, and trick it into healing in a new way with less inflammation, better mobility and better aesthetic results. As I read about it, my heart filled with hope. The treatment works by burning away the scar tissue, literally using lasers to punch tiny holes in the tissue, like some shit from James Bond. That allows the freshly burnt skin to be treated with the patient's own plasma. Incredible technology – and, unfortunately, incredibly expensive technology. My heart sank again when I realised that, outside of China and America, this laser wasn't available anywhere.

For a while I thought about trying to fly to the United States for the treatment, but at that stage I wasn't well enough to travel. If I wanted to try it, we would have to find a way to bring it to Australia.

This is where Svet would shine. She had already won the respect of the medical team in how she'd approached them and asked them to explore new options for me, and really pushing them when she had to. The first time she went to the doctors with some ideas she wanted to explore with them she was totally shut down. We knew we were not the first family who'd asked them to try something – every family that's been through the tragedy of a bad burn wants the best for their survivor. The doctors must be inundated with all kinds of weird demands. So the first time she suggested we try an unproven treatment she was just kind of dismissed. But she pulled out her medical background and let them have it.

'I'm not here bringing you some bullshit skin creams I found on Google. Check out this research: these are the outcomes from all these tests, these were the variables – and I know in Dana's case she's got a statistically significant chance of responding to these different treatments.'

Svet told me, 'It's the hardest thing to get across, that I'm not just this desperate family member, praying, "Just take a little bit more care of my family member."'

We both knew miracles don't happen; we're not stupid. But it's really hard not to come across as desperate when you are, in fact, desperate.

I brought up the laser with Dale, my physiotherapist. We thought that if we could get through to Dale, then he could get through to the surgeons. He's such a well-rounded specialist in so many aspects of burns, and I knew he would have an open mind. I also trusted him. Together we'd endured month after month of therapy – him pushing me to go that little bit further, me swearing and bleeding all over him. We understood each other. I knew he would hear me out and not write off my suggestions straight away. But when I told him what I'd found about the CO_2 laser, he was doubtful.

'Don't believe everything you read, Dana,' he said. 'There's a lot of people out there promising a miracle cure.'

'I'm not a dickhead, Dale,' I reassured him. 'I know how to read a research report. I know what I'm talking about.' I emailed the document through to him and the next day he came back and told me that the laser looked good, but that it wouldn't be easy. The hospital had actually already been trying to get that particular laser for over a year, but they just couldn't afford it. They'd been trying to get government funding but had been unable to convince funding bodies to help them out.

'Every bit of equipment has to be justified,' Dale explained. 'But no unit in Australia has the experience or a history of treatment of this kind, so it's a hard sell.'

'So you need a history of treatment to show it works before you can buy it?'

'Exactly.'

'*Hmmm*,' I thought. If they needed a history of treatment to prove it worked, that meant they needed a burns survivor crazy enough to try the treatment. I knew just the woman.

Svet made contact with Lumenis, the company that manufactures the laser. Because of the intense global media attention they already knew about me, and we started corresponding. Once again, the whole feeding frenzy around my story was a curse at times, but it was a blessing if you looked at it the right way. Lumenis were sympathetic, but they weren't about to give us this very expensive piece of technology for free. We went back and forth with them, trying to work out a compromise. They had the technology and the money – we had a famous world-class surgeon in Fiona Wood and me, a high-profile burns patient willing to do anything to aid my recovery.

In the end, one of their project managers took a real interest in my case and we started talking about potentially bringing me in as a test subject for this new technology. We knew it could be a bit of a marketing victory for them, with all the news stories that could be written about me proving the good their technology could do.

Meanwhile we lobbied the hospital for their co-operation. Dale was a really excellent advocate for us. He would talk to the surgeons and let them know we weren't just some crazy people clutching at straws. At that point, I'm pretty sure that a lot of the hospital staff were avoiding us. Svet joked that when the burns team saw us coming in the corridor they would run and hide, like, 'These bitches again? If they catch us they'll start up about the laser.' But slowly, slowly, we made our case to the hospital.

With Dale backing us up, we went to Fiona Wood, who is basically a god in the field of burns treatment, and she was like, 'Dana, I know you want the best, but there just is no miracle treatment.'

Svet was calm, but firm. 'I don't need a miracle; I need you to tell me what we can possibly do to make this happen. What can we do for you to make this happen?' When she sat down with the hospital, she took off her 'Dana's sister' hat and put on her 'business woman' hat. That's the thing about my sister. She's proof that, with enough drive and determination, you can get anything done.

Finally, with Fiona Wood's help, we were able to leverage a deal between Lumenis and the hospital. Lumenis agreed to lend us a laser for free for eighteen months. For those months, myself and many other burns patients would be the guinea pigs, and Fiona's team would articulate the outcomes.

So I was the first person in Australia, and among the first in the world, to be treated by the Lumenis UltraPulse fractional CO_2 laser. It's a cool bit of equipment: a tall, sleek unit that's mobile enough to be wheeled into an operating theatre – a huge advance from just a few years before, when a surgical laser basically needed a whole room built around it to keep it running.

I've now had the CO_2 laser treatment on several occasions – it is valuable after-care that helps reclaim mobility or graft skin after I've undergone an operation. Like Fiona Wood said, it's no miracle cure – there is no miracle cure – but it has helped immensely. It's been wonderful in calming down the scars on my face, which I'm incredibly grateful for, but it's done much more than just aesthetic improvements. It's helped to slightly release the tightest scars all over my body, which has let me regain mobility. And with the laser added to the toolkit, my medical team have been able to give me better recoveries following operations. It means that they can treat the scars from new operations as they develop, so I can get away with a smaller graft, or sometimes I don't need a graft at all: just a release operation and laser treatments. It really helps restore functionality, which is, for me and for all burns survivors, so vitally important.

Getting the laser to the Royal Perth was essential to my successful recovery, but the best thing about it has been all the good it's done since. The trial period Fiona Wood had with the laser, the tests and work done on me and other burns survivors, it was all translated into research that other Australian medical teams were able to build on.

Fiona and her team went on to present that work and they've been able to demonstrate the real-life results of that technology. As a result, major hospitals and burns units around the country have gone ahead and got lasers. And, I am stoked to say, I helped to raise enough funds to allow the Perth Children's Hospital to purchase a laser of their very own.

It's a real example of how important it is to keep pushing, to never settle for survival. And of how the doctors working day and night to make the life of burns survivors better actually do make a huge difference. They go above and beyond, and that means they save lives and improve those lives they've already saved.

Some people think research of the sort conducted by Fiona Wood and her team is just done for research's sake. That's not true – it actually makes all the difference in the world. I'm living proof of how scientific research can have an effect on a real life. The research being done in Perth, in particular, is being recognised more and more for its quality and innovation. Dale, Suzanne, Fiona and others who helped me are at the forefront of teaching and training the next generation of burn specialists. Their hard work and my drive to thrive have had real, positive results.

And in terms of my recovery, I'm years ahead of where anyone thought I'd be. I can raise my arms up past my shoulders on both sides. I can stretch, I can swivel. When my nephews and niece want to play I can bend down and pick them up. I can put on my own makeup and do my

hair and go out with friends and family and most importantly live and enjoy my life. My recovery has amazed
even the doctors and that's a wonderful feeling.

Once, not long after the burn, Svet had said to me,
'It's fucked up what happened to you. You can sit there
and cry about all the lemons life has given you or you can
make lemonade.'

Ever since then, Svet's been helping me make lemonade.

I was beyond lucky when I was burnt, because I had
my family. Them rallying around me, their sacrifice, having them by my side for endless years – that was the only
way I could have survived. Without them and everything
they've done for me, I would be completely out of luck.

Without them it would have been impossible to physically endure what I have had to. The maddening itch
that didn't let up for three years. Two years and eight
months in a pressure mask, and three years in my pressure
garment. Two and a half years of sleeping sitting up on a
crucifix with splints for my wrists, arms, palms, elbows
and even my mouth. And that was just to sleep! During
the day I wore a neck brace, and two different sets of
arm and wrist splints which had to be rotated regularly.
My jaw was rebuilt with five sets of braces and two jaw
expanders. I endured constant hard-core physiotherapy
sessions nearly every day for five years, sometimes three
times a day. They took skin from my right leg four and a
half times to graft onto my body, the left leg four times.
My groin was used to rebuild my neck, and it would then

take four further release operations to begin to restore my mobility. It was a long journey, but I was rebuilt, and mentally stronger than ever, and I couldn't have done any of that without my loved ones.

Many people in my situation don't have that incredibly good fortune and without a family to get you through, things can be just about impossible. People who have been badly burnt lose everything – not just their looks and life-style but their livelihoods. Survivors of bad burns often can't work, or advocate for themselves, and there are no dedicated centres to look after their special needs. You've got young men and women my age living in retirement homes because those are the only affordable places that provide the around-the-clock care. Can you imagine the psychological toll it would take on a young person to be physically disfigured, robbed of mobility and physical function, and then have to spend the rest of their life in an old people's home? There is a better way, and I'm going to do whatever it takes to help. We have to keep fighting.

chapter 19

A BAD HAND

Of course, no matter how hard you fight, you aren't always going to come out on top. To tell the truth, someone in my position probably loses more battles than she wins. And I've fought a lot of battles, way too many for someone my age. Way too many for someone a hundred years old, really. Every time something wonderful happens, you never know if you've got some really bad news waiting for you just around the corner.

And boy, there was some bad news around the corner.

Towards the end of 2013, I realised I hadn't menstruated at all since the injury. It was a long time, but it's not uncommon for women who have suffered severe trauma to experience disruptions to natural bodily rhythms. I knew one girl who'd missed her period for five months, so at first I wasn't too worried. But after nearly two years,

I was starting to feel a little uneasy and decided it was worth looking at, and I went in for a check-up.

My GP suggested a pap smear to determine when I might expect my period to return, or what the reason for the delay could be. The test indicated that I had irregular cells in my reproductive organs, and so I booked to see a specialist to have the irregular cells removed. Any abnormal pap test result can cause a lot of anxiety, but I tried to stay relaxed. I told myself I was only twenty-seven, and I had already been through so much. What was one more procedure?

After the operation, the doctor told me everything looked pretty good, but that I should come back again in six months for another check-up to keep an eye on it.

Two weeks later I got a call from my doctor's receptionist.

'You need to come in and see us right now.'

'No, it's fine,' I said. 'Everything was cool with the test results, there's no need for me to come back for six months.'

There was a bit of a pause. 'Dana, it's very important you come in as soon as possible.' It sounded really serious, so I dropped everything and went into the doctor's office. My mum and sister insisted on coming with me, even though I told them not to worry about it. I figured the doctor was just taking extra care given my history and wanted to warn me about being careful with future treatments.

Now, at the time I had this really great doctor. He was a nice guy and we had a great rapport. We'd been through some tough times together – but now, for the first time, it looked like he was going to cry. I met his eyes, and they were filled with sadness, and then they dropped down to his desk.

'What is it?' I asked him. 'Is it bad?'

'Dana.' He looked up at me. 'I'm sorry. You've got cervical cancer.'

At this point, I kind of went numb. Like the world had receded away from me, like I was suddenly in another reality. Mum and Svet were with me, and I could see Mum sitting in the corner, hugging herself and rocking back and forth. I could see that she was crying but I couldn't hear her, just a weird buzzing in my ears.

'Really?' I asked my doctor, at last.

'I'm so sorry, Dana.'

It didn't seem real. Cancer? I was twenty-seven years old. How could that be possible? I touched my hair, which had only just started growing back. Oh God, was I going to lose my hair again? I remembered looking in the mirror in the first weeks after the attack and trying to find relief in the fact I looked a bit like a cancer survivor, rather than a burns survivor. The irony was killing me. Possibly literally. *How could I have cancer?*

At this stage we didn't know how bad it was or how advanced. They did some more tests, and an operation was scheduled as soon as possible to have the cancerous cells removed.

Nobody could tell me why cancer had chosen me, but the best guess is that it was a secondary effect of the burn. The cancer was isolated in and around my cervix, and it was a type that can occur when the immune system is compromised; mine had been taking hit after hit after hit for months. The burn, the infections that followed, abscesses in my skin, sepsis. As my doctors explained it, the insult to the body caused by a burn like mine and the constant operations afterwards means that the body is unable to cope with the sheer amount of damage. The immune system suffers in the face of the shock and can't keep up with fighting and still repairing at the cellular level. It's likely that this is what allowed the cancerous cells to form. So, in my heart, I do believe it's the result of the burn. I was the epitome of health before I was burnt, and we don't have any history of cervical cancer in our family.

I honestly couldn't believe my bad luck. I was so physically ruined prior to that, I could not envision any future where it could get any worse – and then it got worse. Svet couldn't believe it either. She was like, 'Are you fucking kidding me, world? What else are you going to throw at us?' Nobody around me could believe it.

The same day I found out I had cancer I was supposed to film a news segment to help raise money for the Children's Hospital's vital laser. My mum and Svet advised me not to, to go home instead and take time to let this news sink in, but I was determined to do it. I filmed the segment, and I'm glad I did because it was such an important cause. But watching it back later on, I couldn't help but notice how flat my eyes looked, like the Dana spark had gone out again.

The next time I went in to have my physio session with Dale, I burst into tears halfway through our first exercise.

'Dale. I've got cancer,' I told him. 'They just found it.'

It was maybe the first time I'd seen Dale look shocked. 'You know what, Dana? Fuck that, and fuck physio today. Let's just have some fun.'

So we put away all the physio stuff and went down to the cafe to have coffee and just talked shit until I felt a little better. He was such a kind, caring person. That's what makes the difference between a good and a great medical professional, in my experience. Someone who knows that sometimes the best treatment isn't medicine at all, but rather just a little kindness.

To remove the cancer, they put me under general anaesthetic. It was a fairly invasive procedure and I did not bounce back quickly. I was trying to stay positive, to keep moving on with my life, but my body just was not co-operating. I'd made a commitment to appear at an International Women's Day event to raise awareness for violence against women, but in the wake of the cancer operation my health started to fail.

I was getting weaker, and before long I was running a high fever. Some kind of infection had set in on the open sores on my body and eleven abscesses started forming all over. One huge abscess formed on my chest, a really painful one that pushed on my organs to the point where I could barely move. The wounds were forming faster than they could be drained or heal. I remember staring in the mirror in dismay, thinking that I was in no shape to do the International Women's Day event that I'd been really looking forward to.

My body couldn't cope. One morning my mum came to get me out of bed and found I was just about ruined by fever. Mum called a doctor and I was immediately rushed to emergency. They got me there just in time. My system was under siege, in total sepsis from infection and on the verge of what they called 'a full system shutdown'. To save my life they had to surgically remove all of the abscesses, which had tipped over into potentially fatal territory.

Sometimes you get dealt a bad hand. Not so long ago I'd been looking forward to doing a charity event, thinking about outfits, preparing what I would speak about. Now I was back in hospital, fighting for my life – again.

You know what, though? That wasn't even the worst news I had that month.

While I was banged-up in hospital, and my family were all distracted looking after me, a neighbour of my mum's complained about my little dog, Killer.

This neighbour had always had it in for us, ever since he and my mum had a dispute over the shared fence years and years ago. Ever since, he'd been looking for some excuse to get back at Mum. Recently things had been even frostier because the media had been camping out on his lawn.

He put in a complaint to the council that Killer was barking day and night. This was just completely untrue, because Killer was a gentle, quiet dog. Besides, he spent all day by my side. If he was barking, I would know about it. But the neighbour was persistent and kept complaining and complaining, and finally, the council took his side.

All that time I spent back in a hospital bed, recovering from my latest operation and waiting for my injuries to heal, I was looking forward to coming home and having my beautiful little puppy run up to welcome me at the door. Instead, I arrived home to an empty house, and the reality that Killer would have to find another home. It felt so cruel. He went to live with my Aunty Mila, who's like a best friend to me and who loves Killer nearly as much as I do, so I at least knew he was going to a good home. But my heart was broken. I'd faced so much, on the scale of things I'd dealt with this shouldn't have been one of the most painful, but it really was. To take Killer away when he was one of the few sources of joy in my bleak days was just so cruel and pointless. I couldn't believe that my neighbour could be so lacking in empathy.

A few months after the surgery, I went back in for a check-up to see if they had successfully removed the cancer, and I was told that my cervix was badly scarred. A little scarring was to be expected, but this was much worse than it should've been. Between my over-sensitive scar response and the fact that my immune system crashed when I was recovering from the operation, the scar tissue had bloomed over my most important reproductive organs. My cervix in particular was covered in scar tissue, so much so that it had closed over completely.

I just couldn't believe it. Now I was scarred all over, inside and out. How much more would this burn take away from me? It had taken my looks, my confidence, my mobility, the best years of my life, and now it might take the lives of my future children. What else could I possibly lose?

I immediately volunteered for a special operation to go in and have the scar tissue removed. My doctors did the best they could, but there was no guarantee that I would ever be able to bear children. That was a devastating realisation. But I still hold hope and believe that where there is a will there is a way, and I do have the will. If nothing else, I've got will by the bucketload.

Would I ever be able to just get on with my life? When would this assault stop taking more and more from me? When would the nightmare end? How could Natalie, locked behind bars, still be dictating my health, happiness and future? It didn't seem fair to me then, but little did I know that Natalie had one more surprise in store.

chapter 20

THE APPEAL

In July 2014, my assailant suddenly came back into my life. 'Assailant' is what the courts call her. I'd prefer to not even call her that; I'd rather not have to think of her ever again. Every hour is precious and I want to focus my energy on the positives. She's taken so much from me that I don't feel like doing her the honour of even naming her, and everything that happened is all a matter of record now anyway.

But she was trying to have that record changed.

I was notified by the courts that Natalie Dimitrovska was seeking an appeal to have her sentence reduced. According to her lawyer, David Grace QC, they intended to argue that the sentence was 'manifestly excessive' as I was not as badly injured as I had claimed in court. They were basing this claim on footage filmed for the *Sunday Night* television special.

Unbelievable. The whole thing was so profoundly, grossly insulting. I was still recovering from the damage she'd done to me by burning me alive, still reeling from the realisation that there was more to come. At the time of sentencing, nobody had an inkling of the further health problems I would endure.

The secondary and tertiary health issues from my burn were yet to reveal themselves when I'd given my testimony, and she was essentially saying that I'd faked my injuries. In an effort to get out of jail, she was calling me a liar, questioning my character, just like her lawyers had done in the trial. I was disgusted. She'd made my body into a prison that I'd had to fight every day to gain freedom from, and now she was going to try to use that fight against me? Outrageous.

The *Sunday Night* footage was about me moving on, becoming a stronger person. It was meant to be a show of resilience and positivity – a celebration of life. And here she was, trying to spoil that. She'd looked at something that showed I was growing and thriving and said, 'I'm going to take that away from you too.'

It was insulting to me, of course, but also to everyone who had helped me along the way: my lawyers, my family, my doctors, the army of supporters and well-wishers who helped me through. Insulting, really, to anyone who's suffered trauma at the hands of another human being and survived. I had worked so hard to get to where I was, and I am proud of what I've achieved. For her to try to discredit me like that was beyond belief.

With burns recovery you get used to endless heartache, though, and you learn that one step forward can sometimes mean ten steps back. I was used to disappointment; but I was also used to getting back up and kicking it in the face.

In the appeal documents, Natalie's lawyer laid out his case. 'It is asserted that the erroneous findings of fact came about because the trial judge accepted everything which Ms Vulin asserted in a victim impact statement provided to the court when in fact, unbeknown to the parties or the court, those assertions were inconsistent with, or contradicted by, evidence drawn from video recordings made of Ms Vulin about the time sentence was passed for the purposes of a television programme.' In simple English: I'd exaggerated my injuries so the judge would take pity on me.

On the first day of the appeal, he spelled this out to the judge – that the seventeen-year sentence was unfair because the effect of the crime on me was not as bad as I had claimed in my victim impact statement. 'The impression is of a total invalid, and this is not a total invalid,' he told the judge. I thought to myself, *Yeah, he's right – it's not as bad, it's way worse.* I couldn't put even a single full day of my pain and experiences into a victim impact statement, let alone the year and a half I'd spent waiting for the trial and the devastating aftermath of the attack.

He pointed to footage that showed me driving, boxing and lifting my arms to around shoulder height. The lawyer pointed out my victim impact statement stated that I would never be able to lift my arms above my head.

'It's just totally inaccurate and his honour understandably accepted that at face value,' he told the court. 'I'm not saying these aren't horrendous injuries, they are. What I'm saying is his honour relied upon information that was inaccurate . . . If the sentencing judge was aware of her true presentation, the sentencing wouldn't have been severe.' He'd made a long list of tiny discrepancies between the evidence tendered in the court and the video that went to air, down to a ridiculous level.

Here's one line: 'On behalf of Ms Dimitrovska it is asserted that these statements are inconsistent with the video recording which shows Ms Vulin participating in a boxing session, climbing into a children's bouncy castle and jumping around playing with the children, and singing and dancing with children at a children's party.'

This was the Western Australian Court of Appeal, and they were asking the judge to watch footage of me playing with children in a jumping castle. Get a grip.

My lawyers rejected this completely, pointing out that there was nothing in the videos that contradicted my victim impact statement, that Natalie was still not prepared to accept the full impact of her crime, and it was unfair of her lawyers to use 'Ms Vulin's resilience and bravery in overcoming her injuries against her'.

Spot on, I thought. I had worked so hard to get the tiny bit of movement on show in that video – one arm to just shoulder height, the other even lower. And even that had only been recovered recently, after an extremely painful release operation. They were trying to embarrass me in front of the whole world once again. At least they didn't show the footage of me singing, though. If they really wanted to shame me, that would have been the way to do it.

Once the appeal had been heard, the judges would shortly rule on whether to lower or even throw out the seventeen-year sentence. As much as I tried to put it out of my mind, to think positively and get on with my life, those days between the appeal and the judgement were hard. It's actually quite difficult to not think about something when every time you prepare for another operation you are reminded of why you are there in the first place. And, as ridiculous as her grounds for appeal were, I did worry that maybe there was something in those recordings that might let her slip away. Natalie's lawyers had produced a legal summons demanding that Channel 7 hand over all the hundred-plus hours of footage they'd shot. Who knew what was in there?

As grateful as I was for how the first trial was handled, I knew that the law was very fallible. There are a million little loopholes and precedents that allow smart lawyers to let the worst kind of people get away with terrible things. Thankfully, after all my stress and worry, Natalie's appeal was thrown out. It was basically laughed out of court. The court produced a 20 000-word document that detailed each of the prosecution's claims, carefully tearing them apart one by one.

In the end, making the judges watch all that footage of me hurt their case rather than helping it. In court they'd played a clip of me boxing, heavy gloves on my hands, throwing punches, and claimed it proved I had full range of movement. The full tape shows just how incapacitated I was. At one point, my upper garment slipped down and someone else had to slide the cloth back into place because I couldn't bend my arm that way. At another point, one of the film crew noticed my shoelaces were undone, and the instructor bent down to tie it up for me.

And my surgeon Suzanne Rea signed two affidavits disproving everything in the appeal. She noted that exercise like boxing is a key component of the treatment provided by the burns unit at Royal Perth. It addresses muscle loss, decreased lung function and reduction in bone density, all of which are consequences of severe burns. I was in the gym every day under doctors' orders, not because I wanted to be there.

Professor Rea also described my scarring as 'horrendous'. She wrote that 'when assessed on the Vancouver Scar Scale, her scars are in the worst category in every component (height, pigment, vascularity and pliability). This level of scarring has an impact on quality of life, both physically and psychologically.'

In her affidavit presented to the court, she spells it out in no uncertain terms.

'My opinion remains that the victim impact statement accurately portrays the impact of the injuries on Ms Vulin from the time she has sustained them. Whilst Ms Vulin has adapted as well as she can to her limitations, those limitations remain. In summary [. . .] the extracted portions of footage do not represent the extent and seriousness of her injuries as I have seen them since the time of her injury. They do not represent the degree of physical pain and limitation and the psychological trauma she has experienced and continues to experience since this attack. Ms Vulin is permanently and significantly disabled.'

The appeal judges revisited Natalie's mitigating circumstances and found that they did her no favours. In the opinion of her psychologist, Natalie Dimitrovska expressed little genuine remorse, except for the sorrow she felt at finding herself in prison. She probably regrets agreeing to talk to that psychologist; they painted a pretty damning picture of what it's like to be inside her head.

'In this appeal, Ms Dimitrovska has, in effect, again unsuccessfully attacked Ms Vulin's credibility, just as she did at trial. She has also, in effect, extended Ms Vulin's victimisation by again putting her credibility in issue, and by advancing unsuccessfully on ground which has intruded very significantly upon Ms Vulin's privacy.'

The judges in charge of the appeal were so unimpressed that they warned Natalie that they were considering extending her sentence.

'If this court had been obliged to resentence Ms Dimitrovska and there had been any issue with respect to the extent of her remorse or her reported incapacity for victim empathy, there is no doubt that the manner in which Ms Dimitrovska has conducted this appeal could be taken into account. Because I consider that the sentence imposed by the trial judge remains the appropriate sentence irrespective of the manner in which this appeal was conducted, it is unnecessary to consider whether and, if so, in what circumstances the manner in which an appeal is conducted could justify the exercise of this court's power to increase the sentence imposed.'

Natalie watched the whole thing passively via video link from prison, and she offered no comments or reaction. She was staring into the screen, cold and calculating. I was glad that, finally, there could be no more appeals, that she would have to serve her full sentence. Despite her best efforts, there was nothing else she could do to hurt me. Every avenue had been explored, and exhausted, and I had won.

I do hope Natalie finds peace in prison. I hope she comes to terms with what she's done to me. Perhaps one day she will learn to become a better person, and be able to reconnect with her daughter. But she is going to be behind bars for a long time before she gets that opportunity. Finally I could move on with my life.

chapter 21

UNEXPECTED BLESSINGS

There is sometimes a silence surrounding burns survival. It's so hard – your body, life and identity change so much that the act of looking in a mirror can be traumatic. Some people who are burnt decide to retreat from the world entirely, to never go out in public again. Honestly, I don't blame them. It's so easy to feel alone when you've been through trauma. But I was determined no burns survivor would ever feel that alone again. And to achieve that, I would have to speak up.

As my profile grew, I started getting invitations to talk about my experiences at various events. One of the first I attended was also the first time I went out in public without the mask. I'd been invited to the Brian Gardner Pink Ribbon Gala Ball, a formal event that people pay to attend, in order to raise money for breast cancer research.

I was quite nervous about going out in public, but the response from the people in that room was crazy, in the best possible way. I just didn't expect the flood of support and love that everyone there had for me. People would come up shaking and crying and asking for autographs. I didn't even know how I should do my autograph, so I just wrote my name. It was a glamorous event – a three-course meal, live entertainment, a charity auction, testimonials and a Belle of the Ball competition, where the best-dressed or most beautiful woman at the ball was chosen.

When they announced I was Belle of the Ball, I was like, 'What?' I think they had to repeat it, and then I was being rushed up onto the stage. I was staring out into the dark ballroom, spotlight right in my eyes, like a rabbit in the headlights. I didn't even have shoes on! I'd ditched them because it had been so long since I'd worn heels that my feet were killing me.

I looked out and it was clear I was expected to say something.

'This feels a bit rigged, guys,' I said. 'I mean, I'm not even wearing any shoes. This is crazy. But thanks!' The crowd laughed, thank God, and the whole night was just amazing. The great response from everyone there, was worth more to me than anything. I'd come a long way from being that girl who was harassed by security for daring to enter a shopping centre with her mask on.

Since then, I've gone on to lend my voice to dozens of causes. A big cause, probably the one closest to my heart, is the Fiona Wood Foundation. That organisation, led by Professor Fiona Wood, is probably one of the most important to burns survivors in the entire world. Certainly it is important to me – there's a good chance that I wouldn't be alive if it wasn't for the work they do, and I certainly wouldn't have the kind of mobility and quality of life I enjoy today.

The research they've done has already saved and improved the lives of countless people, but the potential for greater good is enormous. There are approximately 11 million burn injuries globally each year, which lead to 300,000 deaths. The Fiona Wood Foundation is making the lives of survivors better right now, even as you are reading this, and the research and new techniques they are pioneering will save even more lives in the future.

They share my passion for new treatments, exploring every avenue, not resting until their goals are met. Fiona Wood's vision is to deliver scarless healing, in mind and body. It's the holy grail of burns recovery, but if anyone can do it they can. That is why I have decided to donate part proceeds of every copy of this book sold to the Fiona Woods Foundation.

These days, I do a lot of public speaking. It started as a natural extension of working with my online community – as a way to share my techniques and coping mechanisms learned on my personal journey to assist others who might be struggling – and I soon learned that I loved it. I often appear at schools, women's empowerment seminars, and corporate and charity events. I've even been an ambassador for several worthwhile campaigns. As time passes, I've become more and more involved in charity. Giving back really helps heal the soul and rebuild my confidence. As bad as things have been for me, there are always people out there who still need help and healing.

For example, raising awareness of violence against women is important to me. One in three women in Australia have experienced some form of physical violence, and that's just not good enough. Pretty much as soon as I was back on my feet, I appeared at the 2014 International Women's Day luncheon. I gave a speech built around the mantra and hope that I can encourage more women to 'stand tall and kick arse'. A year later, further along in my recovery and mask-free, I returned to the Perth Convention Centre, and was announced as the global ambassador for a campaign to prevent violence against women called Kiss Violence Against Women Goodbye. 'I pledge to inspire zero tolerance of violence worldwide,' an essential message for us all to spread, and live by. The damage done to me and all of my suffering was a direct result of a culture that is all too complacent about domestic violence, and in particular against women. I want to live in a world where what happened to me will never happen to anyone. That takes work, it takes people to move society forward – both through individual efforts and bigger things like the Kiss Violence Against Women Goodbye campaign.

Another organisation I work closely with, Momentum Forum Events, campaigns for improved health and well-being. They do big events every year, including the Pink Ribbon Ball, and also work to raise awareness around breast cancer, men's mental health, and the prevention of violence against women.

Over time, I've come to realise that my life has been shaped by domestic violence. My assailant was a deeply unwell woman, who'd been driven to acts of great cruelty and violence. The relationship between Natalie and her husband was so deeply dysfunctional and psychologically violent – I got all the grisly details in court – that she'd lost control of herself completely. She'd become delusional out of jealousy and drug use. If you bully someone long enough, they will become a bully. If, on the other hand, you show kindness, bravery, provide comfort, then those you treat well will in turn become better people. If nothing else, my struggle has taught me that. It's a message I work every day to spread as far as I can.

In 2014, I appeared in the anti-bullying video #YOUCANTBREAKME. Me and a bunch of other survivors of abuse – racism, homophobia, domestic violence – held up cards telling our stories and showing the world that we couldn't be beaten.

Towards the end of the video everyone holds up cards that say what they've done with their lives since the abuse, the things they've achieved or their dreams for the future; how they've become top models, or app developers, or heads of charities, or self-esteem speakers. My final card said, 'I'm going to make scars SEXY.'

chapter 22

INNER BEAUTY

Can scars be sexy? To my mind, the answer is, yes, of course! The thing is, beauty depends entirely on individual perception, whether you see yourself as beautiful or not. You can take the most objectively beautiful women in the world – pick one at random, Jennifer Hawkins, Kim Kardashian, Miranda Kerr – and I guarantee you that they have days when they look in the mirror and just go, 'Meh.'

Every woman does it. It's not our fault; the world we live in is one where women are judged on their looks from the time they are little girls. That sort of constant reinforcement gets under your skin after a while. It becomes a part of you. And when your self-esteem is so closely tied to your appearance, it's all too easy to let petty stuff bring you down.

It's not fair, but that's how so many women are pro-grammed. It's something I'm always eager to speak up about, something I think every young girl should know. Don't sweat the small stuff. Every woman has a day when they feel fat, or bloated, or their hair is greasy or they have a pimple on their face. Of course we do. But it's all about what we give power to. A total stranger burnt my hair, body and face off, but there's no way the world is going to convince me that I am anything other than smoking hot. (Pardon the pun.)

For this reason, I work closely with Model Camp Australia, an organisation that nurtures aspiring models to do more than just look the part, to search for their inner beauty as well. The women who enrol are ambi-tious, confident, beautiful, really drop-dead gorgeous. But like all women, they have their doubts. My job was to give them a little perspective, to try to share the journey my body and I have gone on. That no matter what kind of hand you've been dealt physically, it's all about inner beauty.

'Put your hands up,' I said from the front of the room, 'if you'd happily go out in a bikini or a crop top.' Three quarters of the women raised their hands, maybe a few more. I gave them a second to look around at each other and then I dropped the bombshell.

'Okay, that's good! Now, keep your hands up if you'd go out in a crop top if you looked like this!' And then I unzipped my top and pulled it down to show them my full torso, scars and all, and watched all the hands fall and the jaws drop.

If you ever need to give a speech and you happen to have a torso full of gnarly scars, you're welcome to borrow my opener to help break the ice. It works every time. And it helped put the aspiring models at ease. When you show that much confidence in the face of what must seem like a full-on disfigurement at first glance, you get people's attention. More than that, you get their trust.

It really opened up their minds as well, and gave us the opportunity to talk about what I've learnt about inner beauty. I told them how I got to the place where I now am with my body. That, while the struggle caused me plenty of grief, those countless hours of agony spent in my mission to get up and mobile again are what make my body priceless.

I love my body because it is mine. I love it because it works so well after taking so much damage. The fact that I am alive at all is a testament to the person inside my skin. Once upon a time, when I had to wear my mask every day, I'd been so sad because I felt like my very identity had been stolen. I've since realised that nobody can ever take that away from me. I was always Dana under the mask, I was always beautiful under the mask, just like I'm beautiful with or without my scars. I respect my body and what it's done for me, and it respects me right back.

You might think the idea of a burns survivor lecturing a group of aspiring models about self-confidence is strange, but my message is one they – and all people, men and women – can benefit from. I got to where I am by making the most of what I have. The most important thing you can do for your body and mind is to be the best version of yourself. Those little things you hate about yourself might actually be the best part of you. After everything I've been through, you might think I hate my scars, but it's just the opposite. They are cool as shit. They make me unique. Now I'm as unique on the outside as I've always been on the inside. I tell them that the modern day is a very boring time to be conventional, so own your differences.

While I was spreading that message, it occurred to me that if I was going to talk the talk, I would have to walk the walk. In late 2016, *Woman's Day* got in touch with me asking if I wanted to do a photoshoot with them. The idea was to show off my body in its full post-recovery glory – something athletic that showed how far I'd come. Again, as ever, this brought up mixed feelings for me. I was used to being in the public eye by now, but it would still be pretty confronting to share images of my body with the whole world.

At the same time, I felt like it was an important thing for me to do. If I was going to go around preaching this message of self-worth, inner beauty and pride, then being shy in front of the camera wasn't really an option. So I agreed and, after a lovely interview, we went down to the beach and shot a bunch of photos of me jogging along the waterfront in a tight pink crop top and little blue running shorts. They were the sort of clothes I used to wear when I was exercising, before the burn, so it was a bit strange but still very cool to be dressed like that out in public after all this time. When the magazine came out, there I was, splashed across two pages and the cover.

I was so glad I pushed myself to do that photoshoot. Sure, in the television special I'd given the world a glimpse of the scars across my shoulders and torso, but that had been when I was still getting used to my new body. That was one stage of my story, this was the next. This was a celebration of my body and everything it could do. All the ways I could take pride in it and enjoy it. To show that the simple act of running down the beach, enjoying the sunshine, could be a miracle in itself. Plus my scars and my body are still constantly changing and it was nice to update people on what persistent hard work can achieve.

There's no shame in taking pride in your appearance. Every person has the right to be happy in their own skin. I was happy with my appearance before I was burnt, and I'm more than happy with my appearance now.

I wore a mask for almost three years; a beige, faceless thing that made me feel like nothing. We navigate the world by interacting with it – every little thing we do and say to another person is in some way influenced by the way we look, by being able to look at another person, face to face, and make a human connection. Until that is stripped away from you, it's impossible to really understand how much of our lives depends on our faces. I endured that intense loneliness, I fought my way back from it, and I got my face back.

A couple of times I was out in public in my full garment and mask and kids would come up to me and tug on my sleeve. 'Why are you wearing a mask?'

'I can't tell you.'

'Why not?'

'Well, if I tell you, will you promise not to tell anyone?'

'Okay.'

'Okay.' At this point I would look around and then whisper, 'Because I'm a superhero!'

'Wooooah!'

But of course, kids aren't easily fooled, and so some kids were like, 'If you're a superhero, where's your cape?'

'It's in my car. It's my day off. Have you ever seen a super-hero wearing their cape when they're not superheroing?'

'WOOOOOOAH!'

Little kids get it. They don't judge. I tell them I'm a superhero and they understand that sometimes being a hero is just about having the strength to keep going when it hurts. Ordinary people can achieve extraordinary things.

People stare for a minute, then they get over it. Honestly, after a while you forget they're there. A friend once told me, 'I can't even imagine you without scars now.' If you want to stare to learn, that's fine. You learn, it's human nature, and that's cool with me.

Obviously, there are a few haters. Any person in the public eye is going to attract trolls. Especially women.

I can't be bothered with them, I've just got tunnel vision for the good comments and I ignore the negative ones.

All those people wanting the best for me made me fight even harder, but the people who were sceptical or negative – that pushed me too. It still does. All trolls do is give me more determination to work harder. I challenge them to walk even an hour in my shoes and then pass judgement, because being a keyboard warrior is a lot easier than being burnt. You don't like my scars? That's fine. I don't like your attitude.

There will always be haters in the world, but you know what? Haters are all dull in the exact same way. I'm the opposite of dull. I am unique. I was unique before the burn and I'm unique now. And I still have exactly zero fucks to give for haters and trolls.

I could take it before I was burnt, but now I literally have thick skin. Bring it all on. I can take it. I've got something that is stronger than hate. I have love. Love for my family. Love for my friends and supporters. And love for myself.

If there's one thing I've learnt from everything I've been through, one thing I'd like to tell everyone, it's this: love who you are. Love the skin you're in. Be confident in who you are and what you have, because that's what's going to get you through life. We are all unique and that's what makes us beautiful.

chapter 23

THE FIRE WITHIN

When I was first burnt, I said I would give myself five years. Now that time is up. It's time for my new life to begin in earnest. I've still got a lot of goals to reach in recovery, and lots of work to do, new treatments to try – but none of that can hold me back.

I've got confidence. I've earned it. If you meet me in person, you'll notice it right away, maybe even before you notice the scar. Because I'm not the scar. I'm not the attack, I'm not what was done to me. I'm Dana. I was Dana for twenty-five years before the burn. I'll be Dana forever after. And I'm more confident now than before the burn. Don't misunderstand, I never lacked confidence, but this is a different confidence.

Here's perhaps the most important thing I've learnt. You grow up looking a certain way, and you get used to people reacting to that in a certain way. You might look friendly, or mean, or approachable, or like you can tell a good joke. When you are burnt, when you are behind a pressure mask, you lose that. You lose context. Nobody knows who you are anymore and, once that mask comes off, people still don't react the way you're used to them reacting. Everything is changed; everyone treats you differently. But then you realise that it's only if you let them.

When people look at me and judge me, or comment about the way I look, that's not on me. That's on them. I've always pitied people who judge other people on their appearances, who treat them differently because of how they look. That's really uncool. If someone wants to try to bully me, that says more about their character than mine.

I had twenty-five years of believing that the world was my oyster, that I could achieve anything. But that didn't come from my looks. It came from my personality, from how I was raised, from the friends and family who gave me everything I needed to be a strong and confident person.

And that's something that even the most savage fire can't burn. My confidence came from the fact that I knew who I was, knew my strengths and weaknesses, and it carried me through my burn. There was a fire inside me long before I was burnt. It's what drove me and helped me to fight when I really needed it. From the time I was a little girl scrapping with my brother and sisters on the beaches of the island, I'd always believed I would be able to conquer anything.

A scar is the body's reaction to trauma, and for some people visible scars are a reminder that they are damaged. For me it's different. My scars are a reminder that, mentally, I am invincible. I may be covered with scars on the outside but inside I am silky smooth!

I've been on one of the longest journey a burns survivor could endure, just in terms of physicality and regaining functionality. Getting to where I am now didn't come easy; it came with a high price. The doctors once told me I would never be able to hold a pencil again, and now I can do amazing things with my hands. And with the rest of me.

Halfway through 2015, I became an ambassador for Lifeline WA, a charity that provides support for people in crisis and helps to prevent suicides. Every day, they save the lives of people who are going through darkness, and there aren't many causes more important than that. Because I've been there, because I've been through the worst, I know how vital that sort of support is. That's why I was so happy to endorse and support Lifeline.

I volunteered to run in the Lifeline HBF Run for a Reason because I knew that would help raise the profile of this vital charity. Much of Perth still thought of me as the girl who'd had her life ruined by fire. I would show them how far from ruined I was and, in doing so, hopefully give hope to anyone else out there in the middle of their own big struggles.

Did it hurt? You better believe it. But it was really just a tickle compared to everything I'd been through, and the pain was nothing compared to the joy it gave me to run through the cheering crowds on Hay Street. Afterwards, I felt amazing – to show off the power of the body they'd once told me would never work again, all while doing my part to help those who needed it most? What a wonderful privilege.

I ran only 4 kilometres, because my doctors warned me that any further than that would risk overheating my system. Next time, I'm going the full 12 kilometres. I've come so far; a few more kilometres will be a breeze.

I worked and worked and worked. My body tells me it's okay to be proud. It's okay to look in the mirror and go, 'Hey, man! What a fucking legend! You did it. Just look at what you've achieved. Wow! You are one tough woman.'

A lot of people look at my scars and think that I should be more negative, that I should be angry at the world. I say, 'Why not love my scars and at all the positivity that's come from them?' From the moment the flames died down and Denis Ericson helped me into the shower, I've been surrounded by nothing but love and support. My family and friends have been so wicked good. They have sacrificed everything to give me back my life – they've worked as hard as I have without complaint and without a second thought. And that's something that fills my heart with joy and gratitude every day. How can it not?

Same with my doctors. Thanks to them, I've pushed through, endured extra pain, done things that other people have never had the chance to do. I've been able to try new treatments and pave the way for other survivors, and that's something I will continue to do until the dream of scarless healing is realised. I will never stop working, researching, experimenting, in order to push burns treatment forward. Anything to never, ever have another family feel the despair and desperation my family felt. For a survivor to not have to experience the years of anguish that I went through.

The world has plenty of beautiful blondes – what it needs is more beautiful minds and beautiful hearts. I have so much to give to the world, because I've been given so much by those around me.

If I'm ever feeling down, all I have to do is stop and look at my life, to take inventory of all the wonderful people I have around me, and realise I'm the luckiest person alive. Whenever I start to feel nervous, or anxious, or upset, I have a trick that I've been using ever since the trial. I slowly breathe in love, and then slowly breathe out hate; inhale hope, exhale doubt; inhale positivity, exhale negativity. You get the idea. If you're ever feeling down you should try it, and you'll find, like I did, that there's a limitless amount of love in the world. And it starts with love for yourself.

If I stand in my underwear in front of the mirror, I'm happy with what I see, which is a right every woman should have. From the waist down, where the fire spared me, I'm free from scars. From the waist up, I'm covered in layer upon layer of scar, but I have learnt to love it.

The scars and the way they've formed across my body is so intricate and almost artistic – like tattoo sleeves. The way my back and stomach have healed, it's fascinating and beautiful. I love the shape of them.

Once upon a time I'd look in the mirror and feel nothing but dismay and despair. I'd think, '*Oh God, I'm never going to show someone else my body ever again.*' That's changed now. I love my body – what it stands for and how it looks. I'm as unique on the outside as I am on the inside, and that's something pretty special.

Five years is up. Time to get on with living. I'm self-sufficient now. I can drive. (Not well, but that was already the case before my burn. If you see me on the road, run!) I can manage my own physiotherapy, massage and exercise. I can take myself to appointments, and travel around Australia on my own, raising awareness and giving back to the world. And now I'm finally ready to move out and live on my own again.

That said, I'll always be around at my sister's house, roughhousing with my nephews, getting them all riled up before naptime. Or popping out and ambushing Svet with a jar of my scar-massage cream, like, 'Please, sis. Give me a massage, real quick, for old times' sake.' She grumbles, but she does it, and that's all I need to remember that I'm the luckiest woman in the world.

I never chose to be burnt, but through this journey I got to see so much good in the world. Sometimes I speak to people who think there's no hope for humanity, but

I know for a fact that in this world there are more good people than bad people. The outpouring of support for me was just incredible. Plus, of course, the support from the hospital and my friends and family was amazing. There are so many good people out there, and they make life worth fighting for.

That day I woke up from the coma – roused myself from death's door to tell Svetlana that she couldn't sing and was ruining my nap – Svet burst into relieved tears because she knew that under all the bandages and burns, I was still Dana.

When I look in the mirror now, I see Dana. Not the Dana from before the burn, but a different one, one who's walked through fire and come out stronger, kinder and more hopeful.

The other day I was getting dressed before going out and I caught my reflection in the mirror and stopped. My face, after the burns and a dozen operations and what felt like thousands of treatments, is not the face I was born with. But it's better, in some ways, because I've earned it. I'm happy, because I've earned the right to be happy.

I realised that the Dana I now see looking back at me is one I've seen before. It was the version of me from the dream I'd had every night in the terrible broken months after the attack. In that vision, I was whole again, wearing that cute little pink dress and walking into a club full of people who loved me. The same thing night after night, and every morning I'd wake up crying because it seemed impossible in reality. At the time I thought it was my subconscious playing cruel tricks on me, reminding me of what I'd never have again. But when I looked in the mirror the other night, the Dana staring back at me was the one from the vision, the one in the pink dress holding her head high.

I realise now that it wasn't a nightmare at all. It was a premonition. It was what would come to pass once I'd won the fight ahead of me. Now that dream has come true.

Life can be a nightmare. It can also be a dream. It all depends on how you look at it. Life is what you make it. Life is what you spend your time fighting for.

And now it's time for me to live.

ACKNOWLEDGEMENTS

Thank you, thank you, thank you . . . I feel I could spend the rest of my life, every minute of my life, saying thank you and giving back and it still wouldn't be enough. In my heart I don't even feel like there has been a word invented yet to be able to express how grateful and appreciative I am of everyone. However, there are definitely special thank yous I would like to mention.

Thank you to Denis Ericson for coming into my apartment, helping me in the shower and calling for help. Thank you for the amazing, lightning-fast response of the ambulance, firefighters and police. Thank you to the courts and the WA justice system.

Thank you to Royal Perth Hospital and all the doctors, nurses, physios and occupational therapists. Special mention and thanks to my main surgeons, Professor Suzanne Rae and Professor Fiona Wood. My main occupational therapist Rosemary Kendell, physios Dale Edgar and Paul Gittings, and my bedpan nurses Lynnette Barnden and Kim Webber Bowen: honestly, there is a special spot etched in my heart for you all. Not only for your professionalism but also for your kindness, compassion and willingness to go above and beyond. Thank you to Lisa Anne Stewart of L.A. CosMEDink Cosmetic-Medical Tattooist. Thank you Paxman and Paxman barristers and solicitors. Thanks to all the other doctors and specialists who have also helped along my journey.

Thank you to all the survivors I have met along the way and people who have supported me. Thank you so much to my amazing friends who have gone above and beyond the call of friendship. Thanks to all my aunties, uncles and cousins. Thank you to my immediate family, mum, dad, sisters, brother and brothers-in-law, and to my nephews and niece for providing a constant source of pure happiness. I'm sure there are people I've missed but thank you to everyone Thank you so much for making my heart so full. Thank you for my faith.

And I know I've thanked them already but to my mother and my sister Svetlana: I will never find the words nor the actions to express how grateful I am to you and how proud I am to call you my family. You have literally been my everything at times when I was completely unable to do anything. You didn't just help me with all my physical needs, you were also there to wipe the tears from my face when I couldn't, and then to replace them with laughter and hope. You spent every moment with me for years, never leaving me without anything I needed. You fed me, showered me and helped me move. Without you by my side there is no chance I would have made half the recovery I have. Your selflessness is unmatched. Even though life has been tough, I still feel like the luckiest person and that I could do anything with you by my side. For that reason I dedicate this book to you, my mum, Vera Vulin, and my sister, Svetlana Velickovski.